British and Irish Elections 1784-1831

PETER JUPP

The working of the election system in the British
Isles is a neglected aspect of social and political
history and Dr Jupp's is one of the first substan-
tive contributions on this important subject. By
drawing on nearly 100 documents from a large
number of private and public manuscript collec-
tions, he emphasises the most critical aspects of
Parliamentary elections in Britain and Ireland
from 1784-1831, the eve of the Reform Bill. The
approach assumes elections are best studied in a
regional and local context, and a balance is therefore maintained between those illuminating the
contrasting elections of the town and countryside.
Particular attention is paid to the social and economic aspects of elections; to the often tangled
relationships between voters and candidates; and
to the general impact of electioneering on small
communities. While the documents stress these
aspects, matters of a more ideological nature are
not neglected and combine in a rounded treatment of a theme which is well suited to documentary illustrations.

DAVID & CHARLES SOURCES FOR SOCIAL & ECONOMIC HISTORY

British and Irish Elections 1784–1831

DAVID & CHARLES SOURCES FOR SOCIAL & ECONOMIC HISTORY

GENERAL EDITOR: *Professor E. R. R. Green*
Director of the Institute of Irish Studies
The Queen's University of Belfast

published

DAVID & CHARLES SOURCES FOR SOCIAL & ECONOMIC HISTORY

PETER JUPP

Lecturer in Modern History, The Queen's University, Belfast

British and Irish Elections 1784-1831

DAVID & CHARLES : NEWTON ABBOT
BARNES & NOBLE BOOKS : NEW YORK
(a division of Harper & Row Publishers, Inc.)

This edition first published in 1973
in Great Britain by
David & Charles (Holdings) Limited
Newton Abbot Devon
in the U.S.A. by
Harper & Row Publishers Inc
Barnes & Noble Import Division

0 7153 6102 3 (*Great Britain*)
06 493438 1 (*United States*)

Printed in Great Britain by
Latimer Trend & Company Ltd

Contents

PART THREE: COUNTY AND BURGH ELECTIONS IN SCOTLAND

PART FIVE: SOME EXAMPLES OF EXTRA-
PARLIAMENTARY DEMANDS FOR
PARLIAMENTARY REFORM

General
Introduction

In so far as parliamentary elections in Britain and Ireland in the period 1784–1831 involved groups of people of differing economic and social status, took place in a variety of communities and allowed some degree of choice, they are clearly of interest to social historians. It is true that their interest may be limited by the fact that the British electoral system remained immune to the social and economic effects of the industrial revolution until after the Reform Acts of 1832. Yet it is equally true that a new industrial society, divided along class lines, did not replace the traditional structures of landed society overnight: they existed side by side until at least the middle of the nineteenth century. In other words, while the documentary evidence relating to elections in this period primarily illuminates aspects of landed and pre-industrial society, it is still of considerable significance and interest.

To be more specific: the pre-1832 electoral system was based upon the idea of representing certain social interests and certain kinds of communities rather than mere numbers or even classes of people. This was reflected by the fact that in both Britain and Ireland there were three types of constituencies, each theoretically supposed to satisfy different needs: counties, boroughs and universities. The counties were to provide for the representation of the views of various strata of landed society and the boroughs for the interests of towns and cities; the universities were supposed to represent themselves. It is true that many county and borough constituencies were, by this period, effectively controlled by a small number of individuals and that in these the prospects of a representation of interests were doubtful. Yet this does not in my view make the study of elections in a social context a profitless exercise. Documentary evidence which reveals how an individual exerted his influence in a community is just as important as that which relates to a constituency in which various interests were in competition. In both 'open' and 'close' constituencies elections came around with sufficient frequency to provide (where the documents have survived) brief illumination of social behaviour and attitudes that would be otherwise extremely difficult to detect.

The case can be further strengthened by reference to the franchise which in most cases belonged to those qualified by their possessions or by their trade. In the case of all the counties and some boroughs, the vote was attached to property owned upon certain terms; in many other boroughs it belonged to those who were members of commercially orientated urban authorities—the corporations. With this emphasis upon property and occupation it is not surprising that in this respect, too, election documents can be of considerable social interest. This is especially true of the county constituencies where a candidate's success or failure could often rest upon a detailed knowledge of what is best described as social geography. He had to know who owned what, upon what terms his friends and enemies let their property, and the mood of the tenantry. These matters were often recorded in meticulous detail and this can provide a fascinating picture of landed society.

These observations are, broadly speaking, the inspiration of this volume. Its purpose is to place electioneering in this period into a social context, without omitting aspects which are strictly speaking parliamentary, ideological and, in some cases, economic. To achieve this object I have sought to capture the full flavour of the documents selected by presenting them in their original style and syntax.

PART ONE

County Elections in England and Wales

INTRODUCTION

THROUGHOUT this period each of the forty English counties returned two members to parliament and the twelve in Wales one apiece: in both countries the franchise belonged to those who possessed freehold property valued for the land tax at 40s per annum. As to the voters, the lack of an effective system of registration makes it impossible to give an accurate estimate of their numbers, although calculations based upon contemporary assessments for individual counties as in document (13) and analysis of the results of elections suggest an approximate total of 190,000 in 1790 and 250,000 in 1830. The county electorate therefore increased at about half the rate of the population as a whole. As far as the county members are concerned, the property qualification of £600 of freehold land ensured that they were drawn from the landed classes, although the fact that successful electioneering depended upon deep purses and a considerable acreage meant that on the whole they were members of the wealthiest section of that class—the peerage and landed gentry. County elections were in fact largely decided by negotiation, compromise, or dispute between them, success usually belonging to those whose electoral interest was the strongest.

The precise composition of an electoral interest varied from candidate to candidate and from one county to another. In some cases it rested almost entirely upon the possession of property and the number of freeholders resident upon it; in others upon the social prestige and the political inclination of the campaigner and the number of allies he could muster as a result. Usually, however, it rested upon an amalgamation of all these factors. Document (1) illustrates how such a combination was put together in the social as opposed to the political sense, and the attention to the needs of allies that was necessary to maintain it.

Not every wealthy landowner interested himself in electoral matters and those who did usually had motives that lay somewhere between purely political considerations and those connected with their social position within the county. Lord Hardwicke, for example (2), felt that his prestige in Cambridgeshire depended upon his brother's willingness to serve as the county member and the willingness of the county to elect him. Lord Lowther saw his duty in broader terms (3): if men of property did not stand up for their position in elections, then they would soon lose their influence as a class. Others, like the Duke of Newcastle in Nottinghamshire (4) or Lord Morpeth in Cumberland (5), merely assumed that their rank and landed wealth entitled them to command a county seat.

Such was the strength of the substantial members of the landed class in county elections that there were very few successful challenges to their position—which is not to say that challenges were not made. The most frequent were from what were usually called 'independent interests', a term which sometimes referred to nothing more than the thinly disguised interest of another major proprietor, as is probably the case in (7), but which was also used with some justification to refer to the interests of the middling sections of landed society—the minor gentry, the yeomen and the more prosperous farmers. In this latter sense it implied opposition to, and independence from, the dictates of the great landlords (8). Sometimes, as in Kent in 1820 (9), it expressed a kind of local feeling against the outsider and the lackey of party—an echo of the view that county members should represent the independent voice of the nation.

A poll of the strength of these various interests was the exception rather than the rule: a little less than 30 per cent of county elections ever got to that stage. Polls, however, are an inaccurate guide to the degree of competition, as the customary preliminaries to an election often involved trials of strength that precluded the expensive business of taking a vote. The start of the race was normally made when declarations or addresses to the electors were issued by the candidates. When the date of an election was firmly known, this could be done up to a year in advance of it; when an election was called suddenly, as in 1812, candidates rushed out their statements (10). The timing of an election was critical to the candidates: the greater the period of notice, the longer the amount of time that could be devoted to canvassing, an important aspect of electioneering in this period and one that has been somewhat neglected by historians. In its impact upon the social and political life of the county, the canvass was probably the most carefully organised and dramatic aspect of electioneering. The ground had to be carefully prepared, as Ian Reynolds explained to Lady Mandeville (11), and in meeting the cost of the operation substantial sums were necessary. In the larger counties, such as Yorkshire, these were often raised by subscription from the leading gentlemen in one's interest (12). However, it was during the perambulation itself that a canvass impinged most directly upon the social life of a county. Lord Althorp's tour of Northamptonshire in 1806 (14) or William Baker's in Hertfordshire a year earlier (27) are reminiscent of the modern American bandwagon, while Henry Brougham's nerve-racking experiences in Westmorland (16) were not uncommon. Canvassing of this kind brought the landlord and freeholder face to face and belies the view that all the candidate had to do was to crack his whip and observe his supporters marching in neat ranks into the polling booths. Even in the pre-reform era, the niceties of gentlemanly behaviour—such as William Jary's observation that the personal attention of the candidate would make all the difference to a Norfolk canvass (15)—ensured that in many county elections the social barriers were to some extent crossed.

As a test of public opinion, a canvass could be decisive and so preclude a poll. The disappointed candidate or candidates would then appear on the hustings before the sheriff and the crowd upon nomination day, and then withdraw after the appropriate speech. Or, if the canvassing had been inconclusive, the candidates would speechify and then proceed to a poll, as happened at the Middlesex election in 1806 (17).

Polling itself usually took place in the county town and for most freeholders this obviously meant a considerable journey. It was, however, a burden that was considerably relieved by the fact that it was customary for the candidates to provide refreshments and accommodation at the end of it. Furthermore a county election could last for as many as fifteen days during this period and here was another factor which demanded careful organisation on the part of the candidates. The arrangements made for the Suffolk election in 1790 are a good illustration of how 'treating' was organised and it should be noted that half the costs of the Huntingdonshire election in 1826 went to innkeepers (18 and 20).

The result of most polls was predictable in the sense that the majority of freeholders voted in the interest of the landlord within whose sphere of influence they lived or, indeed, of whom they were also tenants. This was expected of them and can be demonstrated as having happened by analysis of the many poll-books that have survived for this period. The reason for this identity of interest is, however, more difficult to determine. It was often alleged that it was due to the fear of eviction or other retaliatory measures that the landlord might take if his wishes were disobeyed (22). Yet it is most likely that such allegations were true of only a small number of cases. Eviction was a costly business and if practised frequently could disturb if not ruin the prosperity of ordinary estate business. Furthermore, the the evidence suggests that the attitude of the voter to the landlord or candidates was one of deference rather than dependence. The vote was often regarded as a token of mutual obligations and it is significant that some voters clearly felt that a vote

merited some return from the beneficiary of it (23, 24 and 25).
A precise statement on the subject is, however, impossible and
on the whole the historian must rely upon the flavour of the
relevant documents of which (26) is one of the more revealing
examples.

In several respects, therefore, a documentary survey of county
electioneering throws some interesting light upon the social
character of rural life in England and Wales, even though it is
unlikely that the dramatic social and political changes that were
consequent upon the industrial revolution—in particular the
emergence of a middle and working-class consciousness and an
attendant political radicalism—had an effect upon more than
a handful of county constituencies. Yet county society and
county politics could not remain immune either to the general
political climate or to the developments taking place in the
cities and towns. In fact the landed classes were well aware
of the implication of these developments, particularly in the
years following the end of the Napoleonic Wars, and in some
cases speculated as to whether the traditional harmony of rural
society could be maintained much longer. The tragedy of
Peterloo in 1819 was one of several events which prompted
thoughts along these lines—thoughts that led naturally to
parliamentary reform as a means of avoiding a direct confron-
tation between the classes. It is interesting that speculation of
this kind was well founded. The Reform Acts of 1832 took the
heat out of class conflict without seriously diminishing the
power of the landed classes. It was not until the later nineteenth
century that the middle classes obtained a secure foothold in
the House of Commons.

Section one: PROPRIETORIAL INTERESTS
1 The character of a county interest. Cambridgeshire, 1802

Pop c 90,000 and an electorate of c 3,000. The Duke of
Rutland and Earl Hardwicke had the strongest proprietary
interests and usually took one seat apiece. At the general

election in 1802 the candidates were Hardwicke's brother, the Hon Charles Yorke; Rutland's brother, Lord Manners; Sir Henry Peyton and the Hon Thomas Brand. Peyton retired before the poll commenced at which Brand was decisively beaten. Yorke here discusses the family interest and makes a note of its friends.

The Hon Charles Yorke to Lord Hardwicke,

16 August 1802

I must now speak of some of the *gentlemen* who were particularly active & zealous. The list of *venison* presents, which in conformity to Lady Hardwicke's request, & with the *advice & consent* of the Viscount, I took upon me to prepare, will point out some of the most distinguished. But among these—I must particularly notice Mr. *Wortham*, whose conduct throughout, but particularly after Sir Henry gave up, was extremely handsome & friendly; & tho' from old acquaintance & neighbourhood, he gave a second vote to Brand, I really believe he did all he could for *us* about Royston, & his behaviour in many respects I must say formed a striking contrast to *Sir Edwards*. Mrs. Wortham also was very zealous & shewed a great deal of interest in the cause; I presume therefore that you will see reason hereafter to consider Mr. W. as one who is more to be depended upon & more sincerely attached to the family interest, than your neighbour the *Baronet*; who, in my judgment, is as false & *hollow* as any one I know. *Jefferson* gave me a vote, but did nothing further. *General Hall* acted very handsomely, & certainly did his utmost to divide his interest between Manners & myself. The Revd. Mr. Fisher of Soham was eminently zealous & both himself and Mrs. Fisher gave the most effectual assistance in that important district. Beales & Vitty at Cambridge deserve particular praise; in short the limits of a letter will not admit of enumerating all those who deserved well of the family on this critical occasion; but as soon as the poll is printed, I will take care to send you one for perusal, & will mark upon it those who are more especially entitled to your thanks & attention in

future. Among the *farmers* however, who distinguished themselves in our behalf, (of whom, after all, there were several,) it
would be injustice not to mention Strickland of Morden, &
Wadelow of Littleport among your own tenants; Mr Spring
of Gransden, Mr Hart of Bottisham, & Mr Woodley of
Abingdon; not forgetting Mr Page of Barton. Strickland &
Wadelow are most deserving of your protection, & I verily
believe that those I have mentioned did every thing in their
power & used every exertion to do away the malicious im-
pressions which had been made among their own description of
people in the county, to a degree that you can hardly form any
idea of. Your Steward Mr Jefferson, has been a witness to the
whole business, & can give information on the subject . . . Our
interest among the *gentlemen & respectable people* is decisive &
appears to have lost little or nothing; unfortunately in Cambridgeshire their power is not equal to their good wishes; nor
their activity on a par with the rectitude of their intentions. The
farmers & middling land owners in Camb. as well as elsewhere
(& perhaps more in C. than elsewhere) have acquired a great
preponderance, & require to be much cultivated & attended
to. Perhaps this has not been sufficiently adverted to; or an
adequate allowance made for the change which has been
gradually taking place in this respect of late years. I conceive
that no less than 500 new freeholders have been added to the
electoral body in your county since the contest in 1780. Jenyns
told me that an estate he sold some years ago in *Cottenham* parish,
made near 40 freeholders, almost all of whom voted against us.
Buller's estate at *Isleham* in proportion etc. Perhaps it might
have been better if in the new arrangement & letting of your
farms a little more attention had been paid to the giving a
certain preference to *freeholders* & their *connections*; for I
observe that out of a list of about *98* tenants, the proportion of
real freeholders is but small. It may be said to be sure, that it is
hard & unpleasant, for a gentleman of a large landed property,
to be in any degree limited or circumscribed in the management or application of it; but it must be observed, that where a

large landed property is connected with a *county representation* which has been long in a family, it must *in some degree* be made *subservient* to it, if it is intended to be kept up; & perhaps by judicious management, the actual value of the estate will not be impaired; especially if a comparison is made, between the *annual saving* in point of *rent*; and the *periodical expence* which may be occasioned by contests, either originating in or exasperated by a contrary line of conduct. Connected with this part of the subject the choice of a respectable, & superior sort of *Agent* in the county appears to me of the last importance to your Lordship's interest. Your steward at Wimpole, ought at least to appear always as a person of consequence at Royston Market, & ought to be looked up to by the farmers in the Hundreds surrounding it. British Museum Add. MS 35393 f. 105.

-----

2 A justification of electioneering. Cambridgeshire, 1802

See (1) for the general background. In May 1802 there was a by-election as a result of the death of the Rutland member. At this Sir Henry Peyton stood successfully as an independent candidate against Rutland's son. Lord Hardwicke here speculates on his course of action.

Lord Hardwicke to the Hon Charles Yorke, 11 May 1802

In regard to the expense of a contest, I am clearly of opinion that no money should be spared to support a family interest in the county, and in answer to your question, I am prepared to answer very decidedly, that without expressly limiting the supplies to that sum, I will take care to have ten thousand pounds ready as a fund for the election. I shall lament your personal trouble and fatigue, and shall think that money might be better spent: but I should think that I neither did justice to myself or family, nor indeed to the county, if I declined a contest on a supposition that after ten and twenty years service, or nearly so, or yours and mine, during which period, we have respectively borne the labouring oar, the county would desert

our interest for the sake of others who have never taken any
pains in their service in either House of Parliament. I cannot
suppose that there would be any cause to doubt of success, and
the only question is, whether at all events to join Sir Henry
Peyton, or only in case two cadidates are started in the Rutland
interest . . . BM Add. MS 35393 f. 46

3 A more general justification. Westmorland, 1826

Pop c 46,000 and an electorate of c 3,400. Lord Lonsdale
virtually governed the county as a result of his great property
there; he not only returned both members, he also supervised
nearly every aspect of county affairs. Since 1813 his two sons,
Lord Lowther and Henry Lowther, represented the county
but in 1818, 1820 and 1826 they were challenged unsuccessfully by the radical, Henry Brougham.

Lord Lowther to his father, 1826

I am not unaware or insensible of the waste of money expended
for election purposes. No fixed rules can be laid down when and
where such sacrifices should be made. Families are continually
blamed in the strongest terms for allowing, merely for the sake
of saving their money and trouble, that Parliamentary interest
to be undermined. A person should act according to the rank
and station he holds in society, etc. If they neglect the influence
their station gives them, their property will soon be found on a
less safe tenure. If bluster, bustle and the activity of the master
party drives the larger landowners from the representation of a
county, the example of one party will be followed by 20 others.
No barrier would then be left to oppose Parliamentary reform.
In our friends and loyal people representing popular people
rests the safety of our borough. How discontented and justly
indignant many of our friends feel in the Government abandon-
ing Westminster, Southwark and other places where they hold
an influence.

In our situation I think we should take the rough and the
smooth. For 18 years, you had nothing more than the dinner

expenses, saving a little trouble at Haslemere*; you have an undisputed right for one† at Carlisle, and Cumberland; the arena is only left in Westmorland and one more vigorous stand will, I trust, settle that question. If Parliamentary influence is not to be looked to, the inconvenience [of] a long residence in the North might be dispensed with any further than looking after your own property. The pleasures of London, and perhaps the mild climate of Italy would suit me far better, at least at this period of my life. In the present case I consider myself doing a duty to the King and country in pursuing the course I do in upholding his authority, and supporting his servants whom I consider best qualified to direct the affairs of State. In neglecting the county representation I should be considered as a lukewarm friend and I should feel undeserving of the stake I hold in the county.

I have made sacrifices of pleasure in devoting myself to study, not only in time and labour, but constrained myself to abandon all extravagance perhaps more than others would have done in my situation. In living on confined means I will have the satisfaction of doing my duty.

Let not possession blunt our exertions in a good cause. Yielding on one occasion will be followed by increased demands. There are certainly a number of persons looking up to you for support; this should be measured according to circumstances. There is no reason why the head of the family should labour and the other branches be idle. Let all put their shoulder to the wheel. Surely there is enough for support and maintaining our flickering influence. Let my brother's sons as they rise up enter some profession; let them be brought up to some profession. Arguments never convince and the one you oppose to me is only one of expediency: though I can but offer terms I shall name them. For you on your part help us in the party contest; I on my part will not call upon you for additional sums of money. Lonsdale MSS.

* A burgage borough owned by the Lowthers
† One of the two seats for these constituencies

4 A clash of views in Nottinghamshire, 1806

Pop c 15,000, electorate c 2,200. The Dukes of Newcastle and Portland, Charles Pierrepont (1st Earl Manvers), and Lord Middleton all had strong interests. The 4th Duke of Newcastle had just returned to England on coming of age and immediately attempted to return a member for the county. The upshot was that the sitting members retained their seats at the 1806 election with Newcastle's grudging acquiescence.

The Duke of Portland to the Marquis of Titchfield 15th July 1806
My dear Titch,

The D[uke] of Newcastle called upon me today to acquaint me with his intention of proposing a Member for Nottinghamshire at the next general election in opposition, as he *rather gave me* to understand, to Eyre*; but I should rather think to whichever of the two present representatives he may believe to be the weakest, or the least able to and inclined to support a contest. I told him without a moment's hesitation that I was extremely sorry that he had any thoughts of such a step, that it was always an unpopular and an ungracious measure to disturb the peace of a county, that I was not aware of any dissatisfaction having been expressed at the conduct of either of our present members, and I hoped and entreated him, for his own sake as well as that of the county, to consider well before he engaged in an undertaking, the success of which must be very precarious and the attempting which could not but be highly offensive to many gentlemen, and in its consequences as I conceived, materially injurious to his own family interest. He replied that he was not a person to embark in an undertaking rashly or without consideration but that he was of opinion that his interest would be best promoted by the number of Members he brought into the House of Commons; that he considered himself *entitled to recommend* or nominate a Member for Nottinghamshire, that he had the best interest in the county, that the county had aways been represented by one of his family, that at present both the mem-

---

* Anthony Hardolph Eyre, 1757–1836

bers were nominated by Lord Manvers, and that he did not see any reason why he was to forego his rights. I answered that without controverting any of these positions, which I desired however to be understood by no means to admit, I should feel myself unworthy of the confidence which had induced him to make me this communication and did I not deprecate in the strongest manner upon his own account the avowal of such sentiments and such expectations as he had professed, that no county would or ought to submit as be told that any family claimed a right to represent them, that in Nottinghamshire there were many families who might conceive themselves as well entitled to the representation of the county as his own, that in fact the misfortune he had had of losing his brother had deprived him of the means of offering any person of his own family as a candidate but that even supposing he had not had that misfortune, I should so little have thought him justified in attempting to bring his brother forward in the present circumstances of the county that was I in his situation no consideration upon earth would induce me to do it, and as a proof of that opinion as often as I had heard of his intention of setting up a member for Nottinghamshire, which with the last fortnight or three weeks had frequently been the case, so often had I uniformly refused to give credit to it and treated it as a thing impossible, because it appeared to me to be the most destructive measure for his future interest that could be devised or imagined. He said he was sorry to hear what I said, as he had been in hopes of having my interest, which he now supposed would not be the case. I replied that I was no less so to have found myself under the necessity of stating to him the sentiments which I had troubled him with, but that I could not with any consistancy give any countenance to the views he had opened to me, nor could I too often or too strongly urge him to reconsider his intention and that I would not despair of his desisting from carrying it into effect. To this he made no other reply than that he hoped, although he was not to look for or was disappointed of my support (I cannot be sure of the expression) that it would make no difference with regard to our private friendship. I said in return, I sincerely hoped it would not and as the best proof I could give of my good wishes to him I could not but most seriously implore him to consider well the effects of the measure he had in contemplation. Upon this we parted, but I called him back for the purpose of knowing whether I was to consider what had passed between us in the light of a confidential communication or that I was at liberty to mention it as I might think proper. He said, to whomever I pleased. Nottingham Univ. Library, Welbeck MSS PWH334.

5 The delicate matter of challenging a leading interest. Cumberland, 1804

Pop c 120,000 and an electorate of 4,000. Lord Lowther had the strongest interest and usually returned one member. The other seat was occupied by Sir Henry Fletcher, whose health was poor and whose death was thought to be imminent. Thus in 1804 Lord Carlisle hoped to fill the possible vacancy with his son, Lord Morpeth, and his brother-in-law, the Bishop, was instructed to sound out Lowther's reactions. They were not encouraging. As it happened, Fletcher did not expire at this time and was active, albeit unsuccessfully, at the 1806 election as (6) shows.

The Bishop of Carlisle to Lord Lowther
                    Castle Howard, 5th October, 1804
I have had, as you may suppose, some conversation with Lord Carlisle and Lord Morpeth on Cumberland politics, and I do assure you, *nothing can be more remote from their intentions* than to occasion confusion in the county, or to adopt any line of conduct that would be personally distressing or even unpleasant to yourself.

As heir to an income of upwards of £18,000 (of which more than £12,000 arises from land) per annum in the county, and connected by marriage and friendship with persons who have long possessed great weight and consideration in the concerns of it, Lord Morpeth naturally flattered himself that, in the event of a vacancy, he might aspire to the representation, but should the resident gentlemen think differently of his pretensions, he will never attempt by availing himself of any association of leading interests to put a constraint upon their choice: possessing these sentiments and wishing them to be *fully and generally understood* in the county, he now means to leave the matter entirely to its own fate, desirous only further to have it explained that Lord Carlisle's letter to me was written under an idea that Sir H. Fletcher's health was *much worse* than at present it appears to be.

Having said thus much on the part of Lord Carlisle and Lord Morpeth, I am anxious, as I trust this may be the last time I shall have to address you on this business, to add a word or two on what dropt from you in our conversation at Carleton. In the first place, as to my visit to Workington, that visit, believe me, was undertaken with no view whatever to county politics; it was merely the fulfilment of an engagement made *two years ago*, renewed on Mr. Curwen's calling upon me during the last Carlisle Races, and only deferred from that time from week to week, in consequence of my being detained at home by a succession of company.

In the next place, as to *my suggesting* to Lord Carlisle the idea of Lord Morpeth's offering himself, I would only ask, were I in my grave or removed to any other diocese, would not Lord Morpeth's pretensions be just as strong? Would they not fully justify him in his pursuit of the object in question? Would not those pretensions, all circumstances considered, be at least equal, if not superior, to the pretensions of any person in the county, your brother, or one of your family alone excepted? and could the electors of Cumberland, or indeed any other elective body, find a representative who would, in ALL RESPECTS, reflect more credit on their choice? Supposing, therefore, which however in point of fact is not the case, but supposing that *I had first suggested the idea* to Lord Carlisle, I maintain that I could not have shewn my regard for the honour and welfare of the county more strongly than by such an act. As I have therefore no inclination to disclaim in the *remotest degree* whatever concern I may have had in the affair, I will fairly state *the whole* to you for your own information, and that of anyone else whom you may hear mention the subject.

So long ago as in the spring of 1796, Lord Carlisle communicated to me his design of proposing Lord Morpeth for Cumberland, in the event of Sir H. Fletcher's death or retiring from parliament, adding at the same time, that he understood from the Duke of Portland and (thro' Mr. Pitt) from Lord Lonsdale that as long as Sir H. Fletcher might be desirous of retaining his seat, he was to be supported mutually by the parties to the *compromise.* From that time nothing further passed between us on the subject till last autumn, when, hearing at Netherby that Sir H. Fletcher was DYING and having *fully* and *distinctly* ascertained from Sir J. Graham that he was *determined not to offer himself,* I wrote immediately to Lord Carlisle to acquaint him with these circumstances, and that Mr. Curwen was the only person talked of as likely to come forward on the occasion. The answer I received was, that should the opportunity then present itself, Lord Morpeth would be precluded from endeavouring to avail himself of it from some difficulties that had arisen in regard to the Borough of Morpeth. This answer I reported to *several persons* who, about that period, asked me whether Lord Morpeth would be a candidate if the vacancy happened. However, on my meeting Lord Carlisle at Naworth in August he enquired whether I then knew anything of Sir H. Fletcher's health, or of the probability of any other candidate than Mr. Curwen. I told him that I had no reason to suppose that Sir H. Fletcher was in any immediate danger, but that from his alarming illness last year and his very advanced age, he was generally considered to be in a precarious state, and that whenever he *dropt,* it was expected that Mr. Curwen, to use Sir J. Graham's expression, *would walk over the course*; not from his popularity in the county, but from the apprehension of the expense that must arise from *any contest,* however unequal it might be. It was in consequence of this conversation that I was entrusted with the message to you. All the rest you know; if what I have done is really blamable I am sorry for it, but I own, as I mentioned before, I see the thing in a quite different light. Carlisle RO, Lonsdale MSS, CL 22/45.

6 A leading proprietor decides the result of an election. Cumberland, 1806

As illustrated above, Lord Lowther controlled one of the county seats and in 1806 the other was being disputed between the sitting member, Fletcher, and Lord Morpeth. At the election Lowther's brother and Lord Morpeth were returned without a contest, Fletcher retiring because of Lowther's decision.

Lord Lowther's Memorandum on the 1806 election

Lord L[owther] being perfectly satisfied with the share in the representation of the county of C[umberland] which the general sense of the county has in so flattering a manner acceded to him, never entertained the smallest intention of interfering directly or indirectly in the choice of the other representative, much less of inducing any gentleman to offer his services with the expectation of his support.

Two candidates have been proposed on the same interest on which Sir H. F[letcher] has hitherto been returned, and under the general apprehension that each of them will so far rely on the support of their respective friends as to stand a poll, it has been very urgently pressed on Lord L. to make a public declaration of his sentiments with respect to the two gentlemen who now offer their services under the persuasion that such a declaration would decide the point at issue.

If Lord L. can by such a step prevent all the mischievous consequences which will naturally accompany a contested election, the ill effects of the last which took place here 40 years ago being felt even at this moment, and deprecating as he most sincerely does the divisions to which the county must necessarily

be exposed should such a conflict recur, and thinking that he
cannot render a more essential service to the county at large
than by using his endeavours to avert this calamity, after a full
and mature consideration of the respective pretensions of the
two candidates without presuming to say that either of them
are exceptionable, he has no difficulty in expressing his opinion
to be in favour of Lord M[orpeth] whom he thinks of the two,
best qualified in every respect to render the county that service
which it has a right to expect from its representatives in Parliament. Lonsdale MSS.

_____

Section two: INDEPENDENT INTERESTS
7 An appeal to the independent freeholders of Essex, 1830

Pop c 318,000 and an electorate of c 5,300. There were a
number of sizeable landed interests in Essex as well as a
pretty strong independent spirit amongst the freeholders. For
some time, however, there had been an understanding between whig and tory interests, which had led to infrequent
contests and a stifling of independent action. As a result, a
movement to 'open' the county began in 1810 and here
William Long Wellesley, later 4th Earl of Mornington,
attempted to call upon it in his contest with Charles Callis
Western and John Tyssen Tyrell. Wellesley's allegation that
Western and Tyrell were acting in concert was to some extent borne out by the results of the poll. Wellesley lost, but
received more single votes than his two opponents put together. Moreover 1,514 of the 5,318 voters voted for Western
and Tyrell.

_____

To the INDEPENDENT FREEHOLDERS of ESSEX, Chelmsford,
                    Tuesday Morning, August 10, [1830]
MY FRIENDS!

I am neck and neck in the course with my opponents, who
have the aid of an unprincipled coalition, founded in alarm at
the conviction of my STRENGTH, to assist them.

My Friends, I disdain such Arts. If I thought I could not win the County without a dereliction of honor and principle, I would not attempt it. I am, however, persuaded the County of Essex desires to have a man of Independence and Political Honor to represent it; and I am determined to afford the Freeholders a full opportunity of recording their votes in my favor, and against the unnatural Coalition by which alone my adversaries think they can hope to make head against me.

I entreat the numerous body of freeholders whose passage to the poll has been obstructed by the efforts of the Constables employed and sworn to protect them; and of those, who having gained admission to the Poll Booths, were sent before the Assessors upon frivolous objections, not to visit upon me the insulting and partial conduct of my Opponents, and the authorities whom they have enlisted in their cause. No artifice has been considered too paltry for the COALITIONISTS; but I trust, that having overcome all illegal obstructions by the aid of my counsel and agents, the freeholders will not allow any sacrifice of personal convenience to weigh against the assertion of their rights. I entreat of them to come again to the poll and to *record their votes.*

Every facility which it is in my power to give to the Voters for this purpose, my agents have instructions to give. I am prepared to keep the poll open to the last hour allowed by law. I rely upon the word of ESSEX to give me that place upon the poll which the interests of ESSEX, the great cause in which we are engaged, and the ambition I have, to become the humble instrument of its deliverance, entitle me to hold. If my friends hold fast to their promises, no power in Essex CAN defeat me.

To my opponents I have but one word to say. Let them dissolve a COALITION which must reflect disgrace upon all who are parties to it, and meet me SINGLE HANDED!

It concerns them more than me to accept my invitation. *Their* degredation will be my triumph. Already has a strong feeling been raised upon the subject. The common sense of the people of Essex is not to be hoodwinked; and to the independent portion of it I address myself, when I invite them to come forward with promptitude and put the brand of defeat and disgrace upon the unjustifiable COMBINATION which has been formed to deprive them of their rights!

Let them come early and in strength to the Poll, in support of one whom they will find firm in his principles and staunch to the last.

W. L. Wellesley

Essex RO D/DL/043/5.

---

8 A plan for organising the independent interest. Huntingdonshire, 1812

Pop c 40,000 and an electorate of c 2,000. The principal interests were possessed by the heads of the two Montagu families: the Duke of Manchester and the Earl of Sandwich, and by the Earl of Carysfort. The Montagus had predominated for some time and it was not until a by-election in 1814 that the independent interest could claim some success when Carysfort's son was returned with its support.

ADDRESS to the Freeholders of the County of Huntingdon

25 August 1812

As the circumstances in which the Nation is placed make it but too probable that a general election is very near, it is prudent to be prepared to meet it.

A right of suffrage in the choice of Members of the House of Commons is one of the most important privileges of an English man; the fair and conscientious exercise of that right his indispensable duty. But the privilege is of no value, unless it can be made effectual to the purpose for which it was given. If a voter is virtually or expressly debarred from all free choice, his qualification is not an advantage and distinction, but a disgrace and an embarrassment. He may be the tool, or the victim, of ambition and power; but he can neither serve his Country, nor do honour to himself.

In popular Elections, it is not always the real opinion or the

majority of the whole number of persons, having the right to
vote, which determines the event. Even where the great body
of electors is independent, a small but united, minority will
prevail against them, unless they can be brought to act in concert, and to combine their efforts for a common end. But this
is not easily accomplished. Where the pretensions and the
interest of all are the same, who will take upon himself the
odium or the labour, of directing his equals? Will they submit
to his leading? And may not his interference create jealousies
and division, instead of cooperation? The last election for this
County has, however, put it beyond a doubt, that a great body
of interest is unconnected with the ruling powers; and it is
equally certain, that a large proportion of independent freeholders with-held their votes upon that occasion.

The electors for the County of Huntingdon may therefore
be free, if they please. Every Freeholder, whatever may be his
party bias, or his political opinions, may have the satisfaction of
knowing that his vote has told for that candidate, who is really
his choice.

In order to facilitate the obtaining an end so truly desirable,
some resident Freeholders have felt it their duty to stand forward, and, regardless of all inferior personal considerations, to
associate themselves according to the articles which they now
publish.

They have, it is admitted, in proportion to their estates, an
interest in this business; but it is an interest, common to all their
brother Freeholders. What elector has not an interest in the
Freedom of Election? What man of common spirit but resolves
in his own person, to maintain it?

This common interest then, is all which the members of this
Association can have at stake. The end they have in view is by
no means to establish for themselves, or others, exclusive influence; not even to procure their own return, or form a party
under a particular leader; but to preserve the system of representation pure, independent, and uncorrupted. They respect
the old families of the county; they desire that rank and property

should have all the influence which constitutionally belongs to it. Their object is only that every man among the Freeholders of the county, who is properly qualified, may have a fair chance, if he offers himself to the choice of his neighbours; and that every single elector may feel that his vote is really of as much weight in the election as that of any other man.

If it should be asked, why a few private men have taken upon themselves a measure of such importance, without calling a general meeting of the Freeholders, or even collecting any considerable number to give it the sanction of their names; they answer, First, that the pressure of the time admits of no delay; Secondly, that the mode they have adopted is much more favourable to prudent deliberation, and calm and impartial judgement, than the best-regulated public meeting; and, lastly and principally, that it keeps clear of faction and party, and of every appearance of undue influence.

They invite their brother Freeholders to join with them in support of their own rights and their own interest; they submit to their consideration and acceptance the articles of their Association, which pursues an honourable and patriotic end, by just and honourable means. Will any man lay his hand upon his heart, and say, "the object proposed, is not of equal importance to all the Freeholders, be their property great or small; to the honest yeoman as well as his more wealthy neighbour?" All have a great and important interest at stake, but especially the smaller Freeholder, whose voice would thus be made effective, and who, in the exercise of his constitutional privilege, would be equal with the most extensive proprietor.

Let it be remembered that, since the year 1769, (when Sir Robert Bernard was thrown out by a combination of the two branches of the house of Montagu,) however respectable the individuals may have been, who have sat in Parliament for the county, they have been nominated by the agreement of great families, not chosen by the unbiassed and independent suffrages of the Freeholders at large. Let it then be considered, that the design of this Association is not to serve this or that political

B

party, but to vindicate for ourselves and our children, THE RIGHT OF ELECTING AN INDEPENDENT MAN IN AN INDEPENDENT WAY. The importance of the object, and the rectitude of the principle for which we call upon you to contend, no man can deny. If a better mode can be suggested, most willingly will the framers of this Association adopt it; but, till then, they may reasonably expect the concurrence of those who think and act for themselves. The plan is to pursue, by means strictly lawful, an object truly meritorious; the object is to assert the rights, upon the due exercise of which every thing valuable to men in civil society, all the principles of our legislation, the security of our properties, our liberties, and our lives; the honour of His Majesty's crown, the authority of his government, and the safety and prosperity of his people, entirely depend. It is the object for which our fathers bled; what the Constitution declares to be our BEST INHERITANCE: what makes us Englishmen. We take our stand upon PUBLIC GROUND; and for the GENERAL GOOD.

PLAN OF ASSOCIATION

1st. To form an Association of Independent Freeholders, for the purpose of supporting, upon constitutional principles, persons properly qualified to represent the County in Parliament.

2dly. The Association, setting aside all party politics, will consider as properly qualified to be Candidates, such Gentlemen, having property within the County, as are entitled to that distinction by their general reputation for ability, honour, and attachment to the Constitution, as established at the Revolution.

3dly. The Association will support, without solicitation, such Candidates as they shall approve, and will engage to use their exertions on their behalf, and attend on the day of Election to give their votes at their own proper charge, and without any expense to the Candidates.

4thly. Such Members, as shall think fit, may subscribe towards the general purposes of the Association; the fund so created to be at the disposal of the subscribing Members. But no expense, other than what may be necessary for his own personal attenance, shall fall upon any member of the Association, except those who may subscribe, and upon those only to the extent of their respective Subscriptions.

5thly. The business of the Association to be conducted by an open Committee.

Printed by G. Sidney, Northumberland Street, Strand, London (25 Aug 1812)

Northants RO, Fitzwilliam (Milton) MSS, 79/2/1-3.

----

9 County resolutions in favour of a more independent member. Kent, 1820

Pop 355,000 and an electorate of c 7,000. No single interest predominated and elections were frequently contested. In this case these freeholders were disappointed, for at the election William Honywood was returned.

Resolutions (printed) passed at a County meeting of Kentish freeholders, at Canterbury declaring their opposition to Honywood's re-election and their support of the election of a gentleman of independent disposition, 11 March, 1820.

1. That it is essential to the honour and credit of this County, that it should be represented by two gentlemen constantly resident therein.

2. That it is the opinion of this Meeting that this County was in the last Parliament very inefficiently represented by one of its members, inasmuch as his residence was elsewhere, and the Freeholders were thereby deprived of that easy access and free communication which are essential between the constituent and the representative.

3. That it is the opinion of this meeting that the conduct of a

County member in Parliament should be at all times marked by independence, equally free from subserviency to any Administration and unshackled by any Party indiscriminately hostile thereto.

4. That we cannot recognise in Mr. Honywood's uniform opposition to every measure recently proposed in Parliament, for the purpose of restraining the career of sedition, blasphemy and crime, the influence of that elevated spirit, which should direct the actions of an independent representative for this great and enlightened County. BM Add. MS 38283 f. 245.

Section three: ELECTIONEERING
10 An initial address to the electors, Essex, 1830
See (7) for the general background. The general election of 1830 was occasioned by the death of George IV on 27 June. Parliament was dissolved on 24 July and two days later Tyrell produced the following document. At this election he headed the poll; a year later he finished at the bottom.

To the Gentry, Clergy and Freeholders of the County of Essex
Brother Freeholders,

As I have been induced to come forward on the present occasion, in consquence of the solicitation of many respectable electors, I trust I shall not incur the imputation of presumption in aspiring to the distinguished honor of representing you in Parliament.

In thus offering my services, it will be expected that I should explicitly declare the leading principles of my future political conduct, should I obtain the object of my ambition.

Before all and above all, I feel it necessary to declare my devoted attachment to the Constitution in Church and State, and to the ancient institutions of the country. I consider that the blessings that this Nation so pre-eminently enjoys attributable to them. But I beg most distinctly to avow, that I was adverse to the first great act of the present ministry. It was an act that divided the most able men of the age. But whatever doubts I might have entertained with regard to it, yet as it has been solemnly adopted by the Legislature, I consider it my duty to express my sincere wishes that it may be attended with all the benefits that its most sanguine advocates anticipated, and render us in fact, as well as in name, a United Kingdom.

With respect to those points, which particularly press upon the public mind—my most earnest endeavours will be directed to the restoration of the prosperity of the Agricultural Interests; feeling as I do, that upon the well being of those interests, the prosperity of all classes of the community mainly depends. I am deeply sensible of the extent and intensity of the distress, in which those interests continue to be involved. I pledge myself to give the subject my most anxious and unremitting attention, and to render all the aid in my power to such measures as promise either to remove or diminish it. An obvious palliative is to be found in reduced taxation. I shall feel it my duty, therefore, to endeavour to enforce the adoption of an economy that may lessen the public expenditure to the smallest possible amount, consistent with the introduction of a well-regulated system of Poor Laws in Ireland, a measure calculated in my opinion, at the same time, to produce the comforts of the labouring poor in all parts of the United Kingdom. But perhaps a still greater degree of relief is to be looked for from a revision of those measures which have been founded upon the very disputable principles of Free Trade.

I am of the opinion that the amelioration that has taken place in the laws of the land, and the administration of them, may be still further extended.

I am decidedly friendly to the final extinction of Slavery in our Colonies. But I think a due regard to the objects of our compassion, as well as a just consideration of those whose whole property, without any act of their own, is thus embarked, requires that the abolition should be gradual. Entertaining these views of the present exigencies of the country, and professing these principles for the guide of my public conduct, should you be pleased to confer upon me the high station of one of your

Representatives, I will devote my sincere and zealous endeavours to render myself not altogether unworthy of your choice.

I have the honor to be, Gentlemen,
Your most faithful and obedient servant,
J. Tyssen Tyrell, Boreham House, July 26, 1830.

Essex RO D/DRb/28

11 How to organise a proprietary interest. Huntingdonshire, 1826

See (8) for the general background. Lady Mandeville was the wife of the future 6th Duke of Manchester. Her husband was returned at the 1826 general election, the third candidate being Lord John Russell.

Ian Reynolds (an Agent) to Lady Mandeville

Paxton, 8 January 1826

My devoir however requiring obedience & not reasonings I proceed to acquaint You that I learnt with some considerable alarm, that there were no good lists of the freeholders in possession of the family. My Lord avoided talking on the subject of the election so sedulously, that I could not ask Him at an earlier day any question; & I do not feel authorised to ask any question of Mr. Welstead: but I fear I am well informed: & If there are no good lists at the Castle, we have not an instant to lose in making them.

The cheapest & most effectual method is as follows. Copies of the Land Tax assessments on each parish throughout the County must be procured from the Clerk of the Peace's Office: As Mr Robert Sherrard is connected from kindnesses with the family he will furnish them as quickly as they can be made & they should be recopied on a lined interleaved sheet & bound in Brown Paper by Your agents clerks. In the meantime He should select from the Clergy, resident Gentry, merchants or Yeomen a list of Persons friendly to Your Interests, to some one of whom the land tax assessment of a Parish in which he resides or which he influences should be sent with a very civil & urgent intreaty that he would ascertain the freehold from the baser tenure; the names of Freeholders, whether rightly spelt, those of the tenants & the disqualification of any freeholder either by nonage su Office* or other defect. He should likewise inform Himself of every circumstance that might influence the Voters suffrage; but these being matters not usually trusted to writing the Agent should name an early day on which he will call for the Assessment. He will then gather all the information he can, will suggest further questions & before he leaves the village will minute on his own copy, the suggestions as to influence or disqualification, & reserve them for the service of his principal.

As soon as these lists are got in a canvass can be undertaken: prior to it, a canvass is at best lost labour but myself I think it worse than lost labour; it foils the ground & drives the Game but enables not the sportsman to fill his nets. But in the interval of making out the lists Lord Mandevilles Committees should be formed & distributed & the Agents allotted to their divisions, & an unity & direction given to all measures, & something of order preserved. I send this diatribe to Your Ladyship express, that You may desire the assessments to be copied without loss of a day. Hunts RO ddM 21B/8

---

12 **Finding the cash in case of a poll. Yorkshire, 1806**
Pop c 860,000 and an electorate of c 20,000. The Harewood and Fitzwilliam families had the strongest proprietary interests, but in such a large constituency and electorate the gentry, freeholders and clothiers were an important element. In 1806 the sitting members were William Wilberforce, who as the inspiration of the anti-slavery movement held his seat by virtue of his own prestige and the support of the dissenters, and Henry Lascelles, Lord Harewood's son and an opponent of government. They were challenged by Walter Fawkes, a

* A legal term meaning being under age or holding a disqualifying office

whig backed by Fitzwilliam and the government. Lascelles withdrew before a poll began.

———

Lord Milton (chairman of Fawkes's selection committee) to
the Duke of Norfolk

York, 29th October 1806

As we flattered ourselves that your Grace feels an interest in the election of the County of York[shire] we presume to send you the proceedings of Mr. Fawkes's meeting, and a list of those leading subscriptions which had this day taken place here.

	£		£
Lord Milton	10,000*	Sir John Ramsden	1,000
Lord Milton	1,000	Godby Wentworth	1,000
Sir William Milner	1,000	Richard Wall	1,000
Sir George Armitage	1,000	Mr. Langley	1,000
Bryan Cooke	1,000		
			£18,000

Arundel Castle MSS, Howard Letters

———

13 Canvassing returns. Yorkshire, 1806
See (12) for the general background.

———

State of the canvass on behalf of Mr. Fawkes

East Riding	Wapentake of Buckrose	118 (freeholders)
	Dickering	30
	Ouse & Derwent	107
	Harthill	245
	Howdenshire	18
	Holderness	24
	Hullshire	152
	—	694

* Lord Milton here represents his father, Earl Fitzwilliam who, as a peer, could not openly participate in an election

West Riding	Wapentake of Staincliffe	143	
	Ewcross	299	
	Claro	61	
	Skirack	582	
	Barkston Ash	373	
	Morley	1,838	
	Agbrigg	685	
	Staincross	356	
	Osgoldcross	540	
	Strafforth &	} 923	
	Tickhill	782	
		—	6,582
North Riding	Wapentake of Gilling West	179	
	Gilling East	22	
	Allertonshire	1	
	Langbraugh	79	
	Pickering Lyth	39	
	Whitby Strand	226	
	Hangwest	92	
	Hangeast	15	
	Hallikeld	9	
	Birdforth	143	
	Bulmer	313	
	Rydale	256	
		—	1,374
	City & County of the City of York	218	
	Ainsty	188	
		—	406
	Total		9,056

14 Canvassing Northamptonshire, 1806

Pop c 130,000 and an electorate of c 4,000. Numerous peers and members of the gentry possessed interests in this constituency; one of the most powerful belonged to Earl

Spencer. In the summer of 1806 the sitting members, Francis
Dickens and William Cartwright, were challenged by Lord
Althorp (son of the 2nd Earl Spencer) and Sir William
Langham, although it appears that each acted individually.
At the poll in November, Dickens withdrew and Langham
was beaten. These extracts from Lord Althorp's letters to his
father tell their own story of the canvassing that began in the
summer.

Lord Althorp to Lord Spencer

30 July, 1806, Northampton

Dear Father,

Richard Harrison is here, and recommends my making a
general canvas at once, which I think will be the best myself.
Sir Wm. Langham has written to a great many more people,
and I consequently shall at least write to every clergyman of a
parish, in addition to the squire.

I expect great support from the Dissenters, but we must be
careful not to throw ourselves too much into their hands, for
fear of losing the High Church.

2 August, 1806, Althorp.

Dear Father,

I am going on very well here; I got forty-nine votes at
Northampton market today, besides several who I am sure will
support me. In the town of Northampton I beat even Cartwright in the proportion of three to two. Langham having got
the Dissenters' second votes is bad, so far as it will probably
induce him to stand a poll, which he otherwise would not. The
leading Dissenters still, I believe, continue plumpers [single
votes] for me, so that I hope the contagion may not extend
farther than the towns.

August 4, 1807, Elton

Dear Father,

I am so tired that I only can write you a line to say that I got sixty eight promises in Oundle and its neighbourhood to-day, and only one refusal. Some doubtful, but most not at home, with whom I left printed cards requesting their votes.

August 10, 1806, Tichmarsh

Dear Father,

I have now finished my first district of canvassing, and, as far as I have been able to make out, I have called on every freeholder from Stamford to Higham Ferrers. Exclusive of the Soke, in which, if I have Lord Exeter's influence, I shall have about 200 plumpers, I have 166 promises out of 300 voters, and most of the remainder have promised no one else.

August 14, 1806, Kelmarsh

Dear Father,

You need not be afraid of my knocking up, for I bear exercise better than ever I did in my life: I was fourteen hours on horseback the day before yesterday, without being in the least tired.

August 22, 1806, Althorp

Dear Father,

I had a very hard day's work yesterday, but did great execution. I canvassed Long Buckby, Murcot, Watford, Crick, Yelvertoft, Clay Coton, Stanford, Welford, and West Haddon, which took me thirteen hours. I called on 202 people in my ride, and got 133 promises, which is a very large proportion considering the number of candidates.

November 15, 1806

Dear Father,

Langham, after a great deal of hesitation, struck [retired] to-day about one o'clock. The numbers were for me, 2,085; Cartwright, 1,990; and Langham, 1,381, I believe. I made so bad a speech at the close of the poll that I am quite ashamed of myself, and it was entirely owing to its being a set speech. We very much overrated the number of voters, for the county was drained very low. I had several more, but the others none at all.

Spencer MSS

15 Canvassing. Norfolk, 1817

Pop c 300,000 and an electorate of c 7,150. The principal interests were those of the Marquis Townshend, Lords Suffield and Wodehouse, and Thomas Coke of Holkham. At a by-election in 1817, Edmond Wodehouse stood against Edward Roger Pratt of Rystan Hall and won with 3,861 votes to 3,289.

(a) *To the Committee of Edmond Wodehouse*

[1817]

Gentlemen

In compliance with your request we William Jary, John Johnson Tuck, Jeremiah Burroughes & John Taylor, Clk. have formed ourselves into a Sub-committee for the purpose of assisting and facilitating the return of Mr. E. Wodehouse to supply the present vacancy in the representation for the County of Norfolk. In furtherance of which desirable end we have carefully canvassed the two Hundreds of Blofield and South Walsham, in which are resident about the number of 217 freeholders, of whom we can certainly say that 140 will vote for Mr. Wodehouse, 69 for Mr. Pratt, and 8 are at present doubtful, finally to secure whom our exertions shall not be remitted. We have further to state to you that after due consideration we recommend Mr. William Norfor of Lingwood, a freeholder and a man of ability and strict integrity, as a cheque for the Hundred of Blofield; and Mr. Norton the Assessor of Taxes as a person qualified to undertake that office for the Hundred of South Walsham. We further beg leave to state to you that we have appointed as superintendants in the different Parishes the most respectable individuals whom we could induce to undertake the charge. They will look after the interest of Mr. Wodehouse in their respective parishes encourage his friends and use their endeavours to bring over and confirm the wavering. They will also arrange & bring the voters to a place appointed as a rendezvous and undertake the care of them to and from the place of poll. We have so made our arrangements that no carriages or other modes of conveyance will be required of the Committee; nor will the Committee be called upon to defray any part of the expence to be incurred by bringing the freeholders resident in the Hundreds of Blofield and Walsham to and from the hustings. We finally beg to state to the Committee, that we are completely organized and ready to commence operations, and that we shall bring up the first party on Monday and the remainder on Tuesday.

> *John Taylor*
> *Jeremiah Burroughes*
> *John Johnson Tuck*
> *William Jary*

(b) *William Mason, Junr.* (*Agent*) *to Edmond Wodehouse*

May 10, 1817

Having taken Foulden, Methwold, and Feltwell in my tour yesterday, I was sorry to find at the latter place that about 9 votes of Pink & Purple had gone over the night preceding to our opponents, in consequence of Mr. Philip Hamond, Mr. Newcombe and Mr. Merest's having open'd a House for drinking the night preceding—an adherant of ours told me that the numerous votes of that town being of the lower order were easily biassed one way or the other by the expedient above resorted to; would not the lex talionis be advisable here; one of the E. Norfolk Serjeants might be sent over and by calling himself a freeholder might always keep our voters on the right side, by being quartered at the *Bell* (our House) towards the latter end of next week; and thus keep the Wodehouse men on the rally till ye poll commences.

Jarmyn Moody, formerly Innkeeper of Bull Lytcham will give his vote to us, if his bill for last election be paid—£15—he now lives at Foulden.

On our own part we can report having got 7 more votes since last we wrote, but the *ungentlemanly* artifices to which our opponents descend, in smoothing peoples consciences when they break promises, have stolen 3 votes from us. I attack'd the gentlemen at Watton Market for their want of honor last Thursday, and made most heartily asham'd of themselves; 57 however stick to us quite staunch—

(c) *Robert John Harvey (Agent) to Edmond Wodehouse*

13th May 1817

Mr. Fellowes I understand, has permitted Sir Thos. Beever to canvas his tenantry and dependants at Shottesham, though he professes to be newter himself, and I believe will use no influence either way. If this parish has not been ca[n]vassed by any of your family, I think it might be with great advantage. Mr. Bourroughes is absent from Long Statton, Mr. John Ives from Tasborough, and the enemy has taken advantage of their absence to canvas the little freeholders, and he has got the promise of a majority of them in Tasborough & Forncett I believe entirely by this attention, and the neglect of these voters by your family or friends; Mr. Cooke has been there & Mr. Richard Gurney; but I believe that a canvas by a Wodehouse would materially change affairs in that neighbourhood.

Mr. Palmer
    Tyce
    Blomfield
    Browne
    Doe

Spicer of Forncett have promised me their votes, but the other freeholders will vote with the Revd. Mr. Jack, (& they amount I believe to about eighteen more votes) if some entreaty or influence is not made to counteract Jack.

I firmly believe we shall succeed in your election, yet I am persuaded that to the last moment a personal canvas everywhere will decide a very large portion of freeholders, and I find that the leading men of the other side are u[n]remitting in their canvas. Wodehouse MSS.

---

16 The hazards of canvassing. Westmorland, 1818

See (3) for the general background. Lonsdale's sons, Lord Lowther and Henry Lowther, were fighting off a challenge from the radical, Henry Brougham.

Lord Lowther to Lord Lonsdale

Kendal, 11 February 1818

It is impossible to canvas Kendal in its present agitated state and yet it would appear as shrinking from the cause if we were to quit it. Mr. C. Wilson, &c. were upon their knees almost to beg us to quit the town this evening; I doubted the policy and remained. In the afternoon the mob made two or three attacks upon the inn and we retreated to the house of Mr. Harrison, but hearing there was an assemblage of our friends at the King's Arms at dinner we went up there and speechified for two or three hours and then held a consultation with Wordsworth and come to this determination, that Henry should go to Lowther and commence his canvas on that side, but that it would be prudent for me to remain quietly here for a day or two and canvas the neighbouring villages, so as not to appear to be driven out of the town. We had a hundred and fifty to two hundred gentlemen that met us on horseback and I suppose about twenty carriages; we were all attacked, the carriages broke to pieces. Sir Dart Fleming had two teeth knocked out and many other of our friends some hard knocks and bruises; our friends still give us the most encouraging hopes of ultimate success, though I am afraid the county will take some longer time canvassing than we anticipated. Our agents are very zealous, in some cases imprudent and others quite ignorant how to get legal advice upon some unforeseen questions, so that I was obliged, or thought it necessary, to send for Mr. Raincock from Liverpool as he has had some experience in elections; I hope to persuade him to give his occasional attendance to the

Committee here to prevent their falling into errors of which I am much alarmed. I am afraid it will be a contest of much expense, but if a prospect of success appears I can only consider it as a sacrifice of part of your property for the preservation of the whole. I hope to send good accounts from the county. Lonsdale MSS. _____

17 Election addresses on the hustings. Middlesex, 1806

Pop c 820,000 and an electorate of c 6,000. A constituency in which the independent freeholders, the government of the day and the City of London had considerable and often conflicting interests. In 1806, the sitting member, George Byng, was opposed by William Mellish and Sir Francis Burdett, each candidate acting independently. Burdett was beaten decisively into third place.

_____

Report in 'The Times' (11 November 1806)

Mr. Byng spoke to the following effect; 'Gentlemen Freeholders, after having had the honour of serving you for the last three Parliaments faithfully and with diligence, I come forward with the confidence of an honest servant to demand your support [some person on the Hustings here repeated the word demand in an ironical tone]. If it be too much for me to say I demand your support, I shall request it with a confidence that you will not refuse it to me. I hope you will again place me in the most honourable and distinguished situation of Representative of the County of Middlesex. Gentlemen, I can confidently say, that during all the time that I have been your Representative in Parliament, I have served you with zeal and fidelity, and never, in any instance deviated from those principles which first recommended me to your choice. It has been my constant aim to serve you and not myself: Gentlemen, I have been the uniform opposer of corruption, [loud laughter and clamours]. My principles have always been to oppose all manner of abuses, and to support every practible reform [he was here interrupted by cries—When did you do so?]. I have been always a friend to every reform which was compatible

with our Constitution of King, Lords, and Commons. During
the canvass, I always declared to every person whose vote I
solicited, that I stood alone and unconnected with either of the
other candidates. I can be responsible for my own conduct and
my own principles, but I cannot be responsible for the principles
of any other candidate. It has been said, that I have played the
game of Mr. Mellish. I have, however, done nothing towards
his success. I have rendered him neither service nor disservice
[No, nor to any body else, said a person on the hustings, you are
a mere chip in porridge]: it is the Hon. Baronet, Sir Francis
Burdett, who has rendered him the most important service. It
is his advertisements and addresses which have given so much
strength to Mr. Mellish. It is the avowal of those sentiments
which have shocked every friend of the Constitution. As for me,
I seek no connection with any other candidate. I shall stand or
fall by my own principles. [You'll fall then—from the crowd.] In
the present situation of affairs, I feel inclined to give my support
to Government, not merely from motives of private affection to
different Members of the Administration—not from motives of
personal ambition, or of vanity—but because it appears to me
the best mode of consulting the real interests of the country. I
repeat that I am a friend to the Constitution, and at the same
time to every reform that is compatible with it.'

Sir Francis Burdett: 'Gentlemen, I think it my duty to state
to you my sentiments upon this occasion with the same plain-
ness that I have always done upon former occasions. I think
myself bound to say something to you about the state of politics
and of parties at the time that I am now addressing you. Mr.
Byng has told you that he has never deviated from those principles which first recommended him to the Electors of Middlesex. What those principles are, I am sure I am utterly at a loss
to guess, as he has kept them a profound secret for many years.
He really ought to have stated what those principles are. I will
ask you, gentlemen, is there any one of you who knows what are
the principles of Mr. Byng, or by what means they can be
discovered? As for me, I consider Mr. Byng as a mere summer

insect, who loves the sunshine [laughter and applause]: but if
he has not chosen to state his principles on the present or on
former occasions, he has at least stated his pretensions, and in
a manner not easily reconcileable with modesty. He claims, he
demands your support, because, as he says, he has been returned three times before, and never voted against you. What!
gentlemen, are we arrived to such a pitch of degredation, that
a candidate thinks it sufficient to say, When I was your Representative, I did not vote against you? Is the not taking part
against you, all that you are to expect from a Representative?
and is this sort of negative merit sufficient to entitle him to
come to you confidently, and demand your support? But if I do
not charge him with many faults of commission, there are many
of omission, which he has been guilty of, and which are almost
as bad. Where was Mr. Byng when those scandalous abuses
relative to the prison in Cold Bath Fields were exposed?* [Sir
Francis was here interrupted by Mr. Bowles, who denied the
truth of those charges, and challenged him to prove them. Sir
Francis complained of the interruption, and proceeded.] Have
not you, gentlemen, has not the County of Middlesex, an
interest in this prison? Is not the County at the expense of
maintaining it, and is not the character of the County concerned in the manner it is administered? Is it not, then, the
duty of every Representative of Middlesex, to attend to that
which relates to the character of the County as well as to the
establishment which it is at the expense of maintaining?
Gentlemen it is charged against me, that I am reviving the old
tale of the Bastille; but it is not altogether my fault if that is not
stopt. It is but lately since that subject was revived upon the
hustings at Westminster, by the Treasurer of the Navy, a man
who was the personal friend and companion of him who was
called "the best of patriots", and who holds now a lucrative

* In March 1799 a select committee of the House of Commons was
appointed to inquire into conditions in the Cold Bath Fields prison in
Clerkenwell, and on 19 April it reported that all was well. Burdett did not
agree and in July 1800 successfully moved for another inquiry

place under Government.* That candidate dwelt upon it as a service that he had rendered his country, in supporting the exertions I made to rectify those abuses, and yet now gentlemen come upon the hustings, and insist that there were no abuses. If my object had been merely personal, and that a seat in Parliament, or even a seat for Middlesex, I might have had it without opposition. [No, No, from several voices in the hustings.] I shall speak to that presently, but shall now observe, that neither a seat for Middlesex, nor any honour that you or the Government can bestow upon me, could ever induce me to abandon those principles which I am convinced are the sole foundation of the salvation of my country [loud applause]. In saying that I could have been returned for Middlesex without opposition, I have at least the authority of the public letter, or Manifesto, of Mr. Whitbread, a man who is nearly connected with those who call themselves "the best of Patriots", and also with those who have the first situations in the Government of the Country. When I speak of that Letter or Manifesto of Mr. Whitbread, I am bound to declare the truth. When first I received that letter, considering it as a private letter addressed to me, I thought it was a very handsome proceeding and felt obliged to Mr. Whitbread for some kind expressions contained in the letter; but when I saw that letter published in the Newspapers the next day, and upon the eve of an Election, then that letter appeared to me in a very different light, and by no means a handsome proceeding on the part of Mr. Whitbread. I consider the letter too as very unworthy of the quarter from whence it came, and as soon as I have leisure, I intend to expose completely the sophistry which runs through it. Mr. Whitbread speaks of his great attachment to the Constitution: I too love the Constitution; and the object of all my wishes and of all my efforts, is that we may have "the Constitution, the whole Constitution, and nothing but the Constitution". It has been objected to me, that I must be an enemy to the Constitution, because, as my

* Richard B. Sheridan (1751–1816, playwright, keen whig politician and a brilliant debater)

enemies chose to represent, I object to Placemen being candidates at elections. Gentlemen, in this point I have been entirely
misrepresented. I never said that men should not have seats in
Parliament because they were Members of the Government;
but what I have always maintained is this, that Members of
the Government should rather come into Parliament for those
boroughs which Government can control, and that they have
no just claim to throw themselves forward upon the hustings in
those few places where seats are given by the popular suffrage.
I have no manner of objection to the Treasurer of the Navy
sitting in Parliament; but as he is a Member of the Government, a Placeman, and a sinecure Placeman, I do not wish
that he should be returned for Westminster. The next charge
that is made against me is, that I do not approve of or support
the new Coalition Administration.* If I ask those Members of
it, who professed the strongest wishes for the interests of the
people, what it is they have done for the people since they have
formed their great Coalition Government? The answer then is,
"We have done little or nothing as yet; we have not had sufficient time to mature those great schemes which were in our
minds, for the good of the people." I cannot, however, but see
that they have had sufficient time to mature all their schemes
which related to their personal emolument. They have found
time enough to mature their schemes for titles, places, pensions,
and sinecures; but have only not found time to mature what
they had promised for the good of the people [loud laughter].
These new Ministers have appropriated to themselves all the
rewards of service, without doing those services; that is what I
complain of. When the rewards of service are thus dissipated,
by being given to men who do not do the service, the country
becomes weak against a foreign enemy; not only from the
money that is squandered, but from the want of exertion in
those who hold high places in the Administration of the country,
and who do not do that service which they are paid for doing.
I will venture to say of one of those Gentlemen (Mr. Whitbread),

* The 'Ministry of all the Talents', 1806–7.

that he does not pay for services until they have been performed. I do not mean to say that he does not pay his men
liberally; but he sees that they have first performed their work
—he sees the beer they have brewed. I should wish that it was
so in public life, and that men should be obliged to perform
their public duties before they received the price of their service. To return to the present Election, I must repeat that as to
the principles of Mr. Byng, I know nothing of them: if I really
supposed that he was zealous for the promotion of what is
essentially necessary to the country, I should willingly retire
from the Hustings and give him my vote—["I believe you have
no vote to give", answered Mr. Byng;—"I believe you are very
much mistaken", replied Sir Francis]. Whatever service I can
render to my country—whatever duty I can perform (without
appearing to connive at a system which I disapprove of) I shall
cheerfully do; but I shall never seem to connive at a conduct of
which I disapprove. I do not wish, by conniving, either to share
the guilt or the plunder."—[This speech was received with
loud and tumultuous applause.]

Mr. Mellish requested silence for a few minutes. He had
already declared his political principles in his address, and he
had now only to repeat that he came forward in direct opposition to Sir Francis Burdett. He had not joined any other
candidate, and was convinced that Sir Francis Burdett had
rendered him a considerable service by the advertisements he
thought proper to publish. He had been always one of Sir
Francis's strongest political enemies; and although several of
the supporters of Sir Francis Burdett had also offered him their
votes, he could not be such an idiot as to suppose it was from
any good will to him, but merely for another purpose. He believed it would be unnecessary for him to profess that he had not
formed any junction with the Hon. Baronet: he did not think it
necessary to make any general profession of his principles. If he
supported Government, it would be the measures, and not the
men, to which he would give his support; he came forward as an
honest and independent man, and if they caught him tripping,

the remedy was in their own hands, and at the next Election
they might refuse to return him. He came forward to support
the best of Kings, and to preserve the best of Constitutions. In
speaking of the Constitution, he would borrow a phrase from
the Hon. Baronet, and say, that what he wished too was "the
Constitution, the whole Constitution, and nothing but the
Constitution". He considered the "Bastille" was a stale question,
unnecessarily revived by the Hon. Baronet, and denied that
those abuses existed there which he alleged. He could not
present himself on the ground of long services; but as he had
almost constantly resided in the County, he believed his character, his independence, and his principles, were known to many,
if not to most, of the Freeholders in the County. If he should be
the object of their choice, he would discharge his duty faithfully
and diligently.

The Sheriffs then proceeded to take the shew of hands, which
was most decidedly in favour of Sir Francis Burdett and Mr.
Mellish. There were scarcely twenty hands held up for Mr.
Byng, either from the Hustings or among the crowd.

A Poll was then demanded on the part of Mr. Byng, and the
Court adjourned till this morning at, nine o'clock, when the
Poll commences. *The Times* (11 November 1806).

18 Treating the voters during a poll. Suffolk, 1790

Pop c 200,000 and an electorate of c 5,000. A number of
peers and landed gentlemen possessed interests while there
was strong support for candidates of independent and radical
mind. This account was composed in 1792 by a London
solicitor and refers to the general election of 1790.

Sir John Rous and Sir Charles Bunbury and the late Sir
Gerard Vanneck were candidates at the last election of representatives for the county of Suffolk, each standing separate from
the other. But the friends of the two former, wishing for their
success, united together as a Committee, appointed Mr. Broke
their Chairman and issued divers orders and concerted proper

measures for securing the election of Sir Charles Bunbury and Sir John Rous, although these two gentlemen could not be prevailed upon personally to join each other.

For the better regulating of the expense of maintaining the freeholders upon the days of election and to prevent the confusion too frequent upon those occasions, the Committee thought proper to issue tickets with the names of the respective public houses printed thereon, which entitled the bearer to provision and maintenance viz: a black ticket to the amount of 5/– for the day and a red ticket to 7/6 for man and horse for the night. However many of the Inn keepers unwilling to be deprived of the prospect of so plentiful a harvest as an election generally produces, came to the Committee and declared they would not accept tickets although they were willing to open their houses for that Sir Gerald Vanneck's Agent had applied to them for that purpose in his interest, in consequence of which the Chairman of the Committee Mr. Broke afterwards issued the following order, signed by him:

'You are hereby required to receive and provide for the freeholders in the interest of Sir John Rous and Sir Charles Bunbury as they come to your house.'

'P. Broke'

This general order being afterwards objected to, another order (a copy of which is hereto annexed) was issued at one of the clock in the morning of the 30th of June, and sent to each publican.

At this election the numbers on the poll were

| For Sir Charles Bunbury | .. | .. | 3,061 |
| Sir John Rous .. | .. | .. | 2,749 |

nearly one moiety of whom were brought and maintained by different gentlemen at their private expense.

The election being finished the innkeepers delivered in their bills which upon being cast up amounted together to the sum of £3,500 for the two days of election only, which supposing that there were 2,000 freeholders brought up at the candidates' expense, amounted to 35s. per man. It is to be observed that the numbers polled each day were nearly equal and that most of those who came the first day returned back with their leaders at night. The Committee much dissatisfied with these charges, determined upon an amputation and struck off one third from each bill, but this indiscriminate mode of proceeding being thought rather precipitate, it was upon future consideration determined, without considering the particular articles of the bills, to allow each publican for the number of men and horses he undertook to receive into his house previous to the election at the above rate of 5/– for the day and 7/6 for the night. And the book in which the entry was made of the men and horses each publican undertook to accommodate, being laid before them all, the bills were regulated accordingly whether the publican had or had not the number he engaged for and the several sums of money so allowed were afterwards tendered in specie to each publican respectively most of whom received the money and gave *distinct* receipts to each candidate for his moiety in full of all demands, but eight of those refusing, have since brought separate actions against the two candidates *jointly*, to which the several tenders have been pleaded and the money paid into Court. Pretyman MSS.

---

19 A candidate retires from a contest. Cornwall, 1824
Pop c 280,000 and an electorate of c 2,700. In contrast to the Cornish boroughs, the county constituency was relatively 'open': there was no predominant proprietorial interest and the independent freeholders and the gentry counted for something. At this by-election Sir Richard Vyvyan was returned and was joined by Edward Pendarves in an uncontested return at the general election in 1826.

Report in 'The West Briton and Cornwall Advertiser'
IN consequence of an active personal canvass for the General Election by Sir Richard Vyvyan, Mr. Pendarves, in compliance with the wishes of his Friends, also commenced a personal can-

vass at Penzance, Newlyn, &c. on Monday last. He was accompanied in his open carriage, by Colonel Scobell and John Paynter, Esq. of Boskenna; and by several Gentlemen in Mr. Scobell's carriage. On reaching the bridge, at the entrance of the town, the vast concourse of persons that surrounded them were proceeding to take the horses from the carriage of Mr. Pendarves, when they were addressed by that Gentleman, who earnestly entreated that they would forbear this testimony of their attachment, to which, as an Englishman, soliciting of his countrymen for the honourable distinction of representing his native County in Parliament, he had an insuperable objection. This address was received with loud cheers. Mr. Pendarves then proceeded to Newlyn bridge, where he addressed the assembled multitude. He said, he wished to state publicly the grounds on which he was induced to offer himself as a candidate for the Representation of the County; and the motives which had induced him thus early, to make a personal canvass in that neighbourhood. A number of Gentlemen who honoured him with their confidence and friendship, and who had had ample opportunities of knowing what was his conduct in private life, and of observing the manner in which, for a series of years, he had endeavoured to discharge his public duties, as a Magistrate deeply interested in the prosperity of the County, conceived, under the influence of a kind partiality, that he was qualified to discharge the more arduous and important duties of a Representative of the County in Parliament. The Kindness of his Friends was truly flattering to him, and however they might have over-rated his abilities, he trusted that in whatever situation he might be placed, his unremitted efforts to promote the interests of his native County, would not disparage the confidence they placed in his integrity and his zeal. (*Loud cheers.*)

Mr. Pendarves observed, that he should not, at this early period, have personally solicited the suffrages of the Freeholders of that neighbourhood, against the General Election, had not his honourable opponent commenced a personal canvass on the same grounds; and had he not felt it necessary to refute the unfounded calumnies which had been so industriously circulated to his prejudice, in that district; and which, strange as it might appear, had, he understood, been asserted so positively, as to obtain some degree of credit. He understood it had been asserted, that he was a Catholic; and consequently, was hostile to the principles and the interest of the Establishment Church. To this most unfounded calumny, he would reply, that the public acts of those who had the best means of knowing his sentiments on that point, gave the imputation a most decided contradiction. It was well known that the Catholics were most strongly opposed to the circulation of the Scriptures; but on the formation of the Auxiliary Bible Society in this County, he was named one of the Vice-Presidents, a distinction by which he was honoured, and which he enjoyed to this day. It was also well known, that when an honourable Baronet, who was one of the most zealous partisans of his honourable opponent on the present occasion, ceased to fill the office of President of the Branch of the Church Missionary Society established at Penzance, he (Mr. Pendarves) had been selected by the Reverend and Honourable Gentlemen who have the charge of promoting its interests, to fill the vacant office. Would they have done this if they believed him to be a Catholic—(*cheers.*)—It was true, that though he was from principle warmly attached to the Establishment Church, he was ready to concede to every man, as his indisputable right, the liberty of choosing for himself in matters of religion; nor did he think a man was likely to be a worse subject or a less worthy citizen, because he worshipped his Creator as a Dissenter.—(*Loud cheers.*)—With regard to the Catholic question, he was free to avow, that though he was no bigot, yet the tone adopted by the leaders of that body, and the attitude they had assumed, were, in his mind, sufficient to preclude, for the present, any further concessions to them. This was all he could say; his future conduct would be guided by circumstances; and this was, he conceived, the utmost that could be fairly required of him. (*Cheers*) If sent to Parliament, he would enter it unfettered by party views or party feelings.

His sole object would be, to promote the good of his country, whoever might be Ministers. To the present Ministers, he thought the country was indebted for the adoption of a wise and liberal line of policy, on many points. He did them full justice, and if the unbiassed voice of the Freeholders, on a future day, conferred on him the high trust to which he aspired, he should cordially support Ministers in every measure which he thought beneficial to his country; as he would oppose them, whenever he conceived they pursued measures of an opposite tendency— (*Loud cheers.*)—These were his sentiments, and the grounds on which he solicited the support of the Freeholders of Cornwall; nor would he desire that support a moment longer than he acted up to the strict letter of this profession.—(*Cheers.*)— Others might possess greater ability and more brilliant talents; but he would yield to no man, in loyalty to his Sovereign; in attachment to the Constitutional rights and liberties of the People, and in ardent zeal for the prosperity of Cornwall—of its AGRICULTURE; its MINES, and its FISHERIES. (*Loud and continued cheering.*)—After a number of observations applicable to the localities of the place, Mr. Pendarves said, that circumstances prevented him from offering himself as a Candidate on the present vacancy occasioned by the death of their late justly venerated Representative; but at the General Election, it was his full determination to appeal to the unbiassed and unfettered opinion of the Independent Freeholders of Cornwall.

This address was followed by loud and repeated bursts of applause. Mr. Pendarves, accompanied by his Friends, immediately proceeded on his canvass; and we are assured that the promises of support he has received are very numerous, and highly encouraging. *West Briton and Cornwall Advertiser* (31 December 1824).

***

20 A record of election expenses. Huntingdonshire, 1826

See (8) for the general background. Lord John Russell was the defeated candidate after a poll lasting five days, at which

1,744 freeholders voted. 783 voted for both Lord Mandeville and William Fellowes.

Huntingdonshire Election Expenses
for Lord Mandeville & Mr. Fellowes 1826

	£	s	d
Bills paid for Favours	1,558	7	0
Ringers in several Towns	65	14	6
Drum and Fifes	38	13	10
Music	143	15	0
Hustings	126	13	4
Under Sheriffs Bill	648	10	0
Town Clerk	40	9	0
Flagmen, Chairmen, Constables	517	7	6
Inkeepers Bills thro' the County	6,834	11	3
Printers Bills	139	16	6
Messengers	30	8	6
Counsel	723	10	0
Agents	1,704	14	6
Assistant Agents	483	14	4
Staves for Constables & Flags	14	10	2
Town Servants [Huntingdon]	43	17	0
Sundry small Bills	269	14	10

Total	£13,384	7	3
Ld Mandevilles Share is	£6,692	3	7

Hunts RO ddM 21a/8.

Section four: THE VIEWS OF THE VOTERS
21 An analysis of voting by occupation. Yorkshire, 1807

See (12) for the general background. In 1807 William Wilberforce, the leader of the anti-slavery movement, challenged Lord Milton and Henry Lascelles. It was one of the most expensive contests in the history of electioneering and one that Lascelles lost. It is clear from the tables that the whiggish Lord Milton was very strongly supported by the clothiers and dissenting ministers, and that merchants stood by Wilberforce and Lascelles.

In the clothing districts different trades voted as follows:

Status	Wilb.	Milton	Lascelles
Blacksmith	62	67	65
Bricklayer	86	116	108
Butcher	99	118	111
Collier	12	27	13
Clerk	130	33	155
Clothier	331	1,081	273
Cloth dresser	43	61	39
Cotton spinner	75	79	70
Dissenting Minister	1	23	0
Dyer	37	38	39
Druggist	3	5	4
Farmer	1,017	842	1,192
Grocer	30	26	27
Gentleman	340	236	394
Husbandman	159	172	187
Maltster	57	66	66
Merchant	131	43	149
Schoolmaster	28	24	34
Shoemaker	93	129	97
Stuffmaker	15	20	12
Tanner	39	35	39
Weaver	111	149	113
Woolcomber	83	110	70
Yeoman	312	403	383

R. I. Wilberforce ed. *The Life of William Wilberforce*, vol 3 (1838), 329.

22 A possible case of victimisation. Cornwall, 1826
See (19) for the general background. Vyvyan and Edward Pendarves were returned without a contest.

A certificate
This is to certify that to the best of my knowledge and belief the Bearer, Mr. John Thomas an Innholder in the Parish of Gerrans, and a Freeholder, intended to vote at the last Election

for Sir Richard Rawlinson Vyvyan Baronet and John Hearle
Tremayne Esqr. and that I have reason to believe that he incurred the displeasure of some of the opposite party on account
of this his determination, and suffered a loss by their withdraw-
ing their custom from his house.
Dated at Gerrans this 24th day of July 1826.

> *Wm. Baker*, Rector of Gerrans

Cornwall RO, Vyvyan MSS, 22N/BO/36/44/18

23 An offer from a freeholder. Caernarvonshire, c 1789–90

Pop c 40,000 and an electorate of c 500. Sir Robert Williams,
9th Baronet, was returned for the county in 1790, with the
support of his step-brother, Lord Bukeley, and held it without
much trouble until 1826. Our miller may or may not have
been successful in his object, but he certainly was not called
upon to cast a vote as there was no poll during the period
when Williams was MP.

Richard Ellis of Puilly Bardd to Sir Robert Williams (nd but c 1789–90)

Richd. late of Feien but now of Puilly Bardd near Llanbeblii,
by occupation a Miller says, that he has two sufficient votes at
his command the which he will insure to poll for Sir Robert
Williams at the next election for the county of Carnarvon—on
condition of having a corn mill upon a fair rent either in the
County of Anglesey or Carnarvon. NLW MSS 10338E.

24 A voter pursues a candidate's promises. Cornwall, 1826

See (22).

George Milford to Sir Richard Vyvyan

Poulruan. November the 7 1826
Sir Richard Vyvyan i hope you will indever to com forth
with your promes to My Brother mr William Prior when you

Was at my house in poulruan as I am shoure that it tis in your
pour to due any thing What you like to due i hope your Oner
Will Sir anser me this to my request for I hope Sir there is no
roume for Excuse Mr Prior Sent to you him self but you Never
ansered it Sir hee being a man Worthery of any bearth what
ever your Oner ples to place him in.

    I am Sir your hombel Servent
         George Milford
Ples Sir to drect for me in Poulruan Neer fowey Cornwell
Vyvyan MSS.

25 A freeholder's view of his rights. Lincolnshire, 1797

Pop c 200,000 and an electorate of c 5,000. A number of
families had strong interests in the county, including the
Heathcotes who were said to own one of the largest estates.
At the 1796 general election, Heathcote and Robert Vyner
were returned without a contest.

 Robert Low (an ironmonger) to Sir Gilbert Heathcote
         Lincoln, Aug 8th 1797

As I am free of the County of Lincoln, and had engaged to
serve you with my vote and interest at the late general Election,
in case Sr. John Thorold had stood the Poll against you, I hope
it may not be deemed an Act of Impertinence in me if I take the
liberty of addressing you upon a subject which very materially
interests both myself and Family who are numerous. The
occasion of my troubling you is this. My eldest son, whose name
is John, having signified a Disposition to go to Sea about the
beginning of this War, I indulged his wishes, and thro' the
interest of Lord Hobart got him appointed Midshipman on
board the Invincible, the Honble. Captain Thos. Pakenham,
Commander, who is a relation of Lord Hobart's and who
promised to get my son promoted the first opportunity. In this
situation Lord Hobart left him on his departure to Madras;
accordingly he made it his study to serve Capt. Pakenham as
much as was in his Power, acting as Captain's Clerk at all
Times, and officiating as Aid du Camp in the Battle of the first

of June, which Lord Howe had with the French and in which the Juste struck to the Invincible: Capt. Pakenham was then removed to the Juste in which my son has also served him as Clerk in Consequence of repeated Assurances of being appointed *Purser* of some ship in a short time, and of being told that by a Regulation of Lord Spencer's* the Pursers are to be men who have served the office of Captain's Clerk: Unfortunately, however, for him, the Juste is lately *paid off*, and his Captain is appointed Surveyor-General of the Ordnance in Ireland. In Consequence of this accident my son wrote to Lord Spencer to know if application had been made for his promotion, and had been informed by Way of answer that his name stands on the list of Candidates for a Purser's Warrant, but that there are some prior Engagements. In this Predicament my son is at a loss whether he should seek a fresh Appointment in some other Ship and run the risk of going abroad, and losing the Pursership, or make Interest with Lord Spencer, by the Intercession of an Independent Member of Parliament, to get the Purser's Warrant made out as *soon as possible*, and wait for the appointment. Now it appears to me much more elegible that the latter be attempted to be effected, particularly as I have had frequent occasion to make remittances to my son to supply the deficiencies of his salary, which if longer continued will prove detrimental to the rest of my Family. This being the case, may I, Sir Gilbert, take the liberty of Petitioning, (provided you have no particular objection to make a request of Lord Spencer) to intercede for me in getting the Purser's Warrant made out as *soon as possible*?

As I am a total stranger to you, it will be necessary for you to be assured of the veracity of the facts above stated; for which Purpose I beg leave to refer you to H. Hutton Esq. Mr. Rutter, Attorney at Law, or any other of your Friends at Lincoln. Indeed I should not have presumed upon this Liberty, had not your general Character of being well disposed encouraged me in it. Lincs RO Ancaster MSS 3Anc. 9/5/17. ———

* First Lord of the Admiralty, 1794–1801.

26 A vote disturbs the relationship between landlord and tenant. Bedfordshire, 1807

Pop c 65,000 and an electorate of c 2,100. The Duke of Bedford had the strongest interest and at this election supported General Fitzpatrick; Francis Pym and John Osborn (son of Sir George) both had substantial personal interests. The poll lasted twelve days and resulted in Osborn's defeat; Fitzpatrick and Pym acting in harness.

John Chase to the Marquis of Bute

Luton, 21 May, 1807

I hope you will excuse the liberty I have taken by submitting my conduct to your Lordship's consideration, as to the part I have taken in the unpleasant contest for our county, expecting from the treatment I have already met with from Mr. Brown, I shall have no chance of a fair statement of the true matters of fact from him, as his zeal for the cause carries him beyond his reason & the truth. I have been in habits of intimacy with Sir George Osborn's family for some 7 years, dining with him often and staying at his House on shooting and other Parties. My father was always upon a friendly footing with him too; and knowing your Lordship and Sir George were always friendly, I hoped all was right now. On the preceeding Saturday to the nomination Mr. Brown called at my House (Mrs. Chase was present) and told me he had received a letter from your Lordship that morning requesting we would suspend our votes. I asked him if he thought it was likely anybody would come forward? He said he thought there would (indeed Mr. Sampson told me the day before that he had seen the Marquis of Tavistock at Dunstable and that General Fitzpatrick was the person) that was all that passed between me and Mr. Brown and he wished me good morning.

The next day (Sunday) coming from Church Mr. Sampson told me all was peace in our county, that General Fitzpatrick had declined. The next morning early I set off from home on a journey through Cambridgeshire and Essex and did not return

c

till the Saturday afternoon when Mr. Harrison and Mr. Brett called upon me for my taxes and told me that General F[itzpatrick] had again come forward and that the town and neighbourhood had been canvassed and that they believed every vote was engaged except mine for the General and Mr. Pym and that they felt for the unpleasant situation I was placed in, well knowing my acquantance with Sir George's family. I told them I was extremely hurt at their information, particularly as *yourself* and all my neighbours were on the contrary side. However I was relieved from my present embarrassement; I told them I was going from home again the next morning on a journey (which was the truth) for a week, and as the election was to come on the following Monday, it would be all over before I returned, nor would I leave a trace behind where I could be found. I returned home on Saturday night the 16th where I expected to meet some friends from having an appointment; or I would have gone to Bath and staid 'till the election was over, without letting anyone know where I was. However a friend, Mayor Hawkins who married a niece of mine was then at Lawrence End on a visit and got information of my return, immediately acquainted Sir George and his friends and two or three expresses were sent to me from them. Consequently in point of honor I was obliged to go to Bedford the next day, as I had supported him in his two former elections and had written him a congratulatory letter on his last return, informing him I would certainly have supported him had there been occasion— I will therefore leave it to your Lordship's candor to judge how I could act otherwise. But as to any other interference I do positively affirm that I have not asked any person for their vote either directly or indirectly; I was told on my return home on the Saturday before the election that my Sheperd and several others were going to vote for Fitzpatrick and Pym, who I could have influenced (being under greater obligation to me then anyone else). I said nothing to them to prevent their going. When at Bedford Mr. Brown came up to me very warmly & said,

'Well Sir you have polled!'

'Yes',

'And for Mr. Osborne'

'I have Sir,' then says he 'you are not a man of your word; you promised me your vote!'

'I deny it Sir'

'I can prove it by 20 witnesses.'

Says I, 'Mr. Brown how dare you assert such a falsehood. You have never seen me since the morning you called at my House to inform me of the contents of your Lordship's letter 'till you now see me on this ground.'

He then began to threaten me by telling me I must take the consequence.

'Oh,' says I, 'Mr. Brown, that mode of proceeding will never do with me. I have an independent spirit and will not be dictated to by you, nor can you frighten me by your threats. I have acted according to the dictates of my conscience—if I had acted otherwise I should despise myself.'

I met him again yesterday & he told me I was not a man of my word & he would always tell me so. I will take the most solemn oath that can be administered to me, and so will Mrs. Chase that I never promised him my vote, nor did he aske me for it 'till I received a note from Mr. Sampson on Sunday evening last the 18th after the expresses I received from Sir George.

I therefore well know that Mr. Brown will thwart me in everything in his power (for what I have done) in every little concern between me and your Lordship, respecting tythes, lands etc., and it would give me great satisfaction to know whether it would be with your Lordship's approbation.

If your Lordship thinks I have forfeited (by my conduct on this occasion) every claim upon you to continue the indulgences you have kindly granted to me, such as angling in the Park, sporting over your grounds, or attending your family professionally at the Park I will relinquish them with greater satisfaction than I could cancel my honor and integrity. I have too high an opinion of your Lordship's candor and discernment between right and wrong to do me an injury—and if your Lordship will condescend to return me an answer, that I may know how I stand in your good opinion of me, it will give the highest satisfaction to

yr Lordship's
much obliged & obt. servant
John Chase

P.S. I hope the Marchioness is better in health.

Bedford CRO G/DIDA 146/5

Section five

27 A contemporary account of the Hertfordshire by-election of February 1805

The population of the county was c 100,000 and there were c 2,500 voters. There was a plethora of electoral interests and the conflict between them encouraged an independent spirit amongst the freeholders. The by-election, caused by the death of the Hon Peniston Lamb, was contested between William Baker and the Hon Thomas Brand.

William Baker to his son, William   22 February 1805

One of your sisters has written by this same conveyance, and probably at some length on a subject which has interested us all in a high degree for the last month. The enclosed papers etc. will throw some light on the progress and on the result of the business alluded to.

Mr. Lamb, who had been in a declining way for some time, died at Brocket Hall early on the morning of the 24th of January—I had arrived in town that morning, to transact some private business, without knowing it. Indeed, the intelligence did not reach me till seven in the evening—I knew not who of my friends were in town—but I decided at once to wait on T. Dorrien, had a long conference with him, and made such arrangements as were thought necessary, by sending expresses into the country to Sir John Sebright, Muthertie, Sir A. Hume etc. etc. Lloyd in the mean time, with others, had instantly canvassed the town of Hertford, with the utmost success in my

favour, my advertisement was sent without delay to the prin-
ters, and I became a candidate in due form. On my arrival in
town I had found a note from Pitt, the Minister, desiring to see
me at half past eleven on the 25th ... He entered cordially into
my situation and that of our county, and in the most handsome
manner offered me every supoort which it was in the power of
Government to give, if I had thoughts of becoming a candidate.
This had been previously decided on my part, by my address to
the Freeholders having already been transmitted to the Press.
We entered critically into an analysis of the various interests of
the county, in the course of which I gave him some amusing
anecdotes, and he received much information which he was not
possessed of before. Who were likely to become my opponents?
W. Lamb occurred, as not improbable, grounding possibly his
principal pretensions on his late domestic loss, and being a
person who might be supposed not disagreeable to the Lord
Lieutenant, and other leading interests, such as Lord Grimston,
Hale, etc. Halsey (late Whately) was too fresh in his newly
acquired fortune and name, to represent what has been called
with more consequence than it ever merited, the Halsey
interest. Brand who became the candidate against me, and had
been canvassing already in the county, insciente sese was the
most likely person who occurred to me. The violent Dissenters
had supported him at Cambridge in 1802, and would probably
have adopted him then against me, if he had not been then
engaged, though without the least chance of success. It was
hardly to be expected however that Lord Salisbury, in a contest between Brand and me, and especially after what had
passed at the election in 1802, and what had happened since to
himself, in the loss of his White Wand,* would be very sanguine
for either candidate. But herein we calculated very ill on the
passions of the human mind, and made not sufficient allowance
for the unforgiving temper of an angry woman—'*Furens quid
faemina possit*'. With this encouragement in Downing Street,
but much more relying on the justice of my cause, and the known

* The post of Lord Chamberlain in the King's household.

steadiness of my friends, I resolved to embark heartily in the contest, and to spare no pains to accomplish the object. The whole of the 25th was passed in London, but not idly. Letters were written by me without end—Messengers to all quarters. Among the persons particularly addressed, besides intimate friends, were the Earl of *Bridgwater*, Lords *Clarendon*, *Essex* and *Grimston*, from all of whom I received the most cordial assurances of support. In the mean time Lady Spencer at St. Albans, and in that quarter, (Lord Spencer, though of late connected with the Opposition, still retaining his personal regard for me,) Sir John Sebright, Dorrien and Ld. Bridgewater and Dacourt with others, Muthertie, Dr. Heath, and others in Odsey and Edwinstree, Hy. Baker at Stevenage, Mrs. Milles and your uncle Edward at Sabridgeworth, Mr. Houblon, Mr. Leightenhouse at Stortford, Burr Dickenson and others at Ware, besides the decisive exertions of Sir A. Hume and V. G. Prescott in Hoddesdon, Wormley, Broxbourn, Cheshunt and Waltham, and many active zealous friends in various other quarters having paved the way for a successful issue of the contest. Still, however, a personal canvass through the county was absolutely necessary, and this at a season of the year far from favourable, and my own health hardly equal to the fatigue. The ground was covered with snow, and all the cross lanes so choked up, as to be hardly passable on horseback—and even the communication from town to town on the high road in some places very bad particularly between St. Albans and Great Berkhamsted. However, on the back of the gallant Pumpkin, (my chaise attending me as it could at intervals by the great roads, and meeting me at the places where I was to sleep,) I happily accomplished this fatiguing canvass, in which however much arrangement was required, so as to take the Market days of each respective large town. This, however, not being practicable in all instances, the defect was to be, and was, manfully supplied by the activity of my friends. I had other difficulties to encounter of which I shall give you, before I have done, a short account. In the mean time my days on the canvass were thus disposed. I reached Hertford on Saturday, the 26th, and went round that town with Lloyd and others without delay. Every thing here bore the most flattering appearance. I made an arrangement at the same time with Dickenson Burr and others to canvass Ware on the Monday (the 28th) Sunday being dedicated to quiet at home, and to the writing and receiving letters, sending messengers etc. At Ware my canvass was almost as flattering as at Hertford—Byde and Plumer *stating themselves neutral*, and the large bulk of the freeholders there, and elsewhere, except in Hitchen and Royston, having come to their senses since 1802. Passing from Ware, I took Watton, where every vote was now in my favour, though in 1802 they had been as decidedly adverse. Harry Baker received me at dinner and for the night, and I had nothing to do the next morning but to go round Stevenage and thank the voters for their promises already made in my favour to their Rector. From Stevenage we proceeded (H.B. and I) to Hitchin. This place under the influence of Hale, who joined with Hatfield House in supporting Brand, was generally adverse. Wilshere too had here poisoned their minds, and from these circumstances you will perceive this is the Hundred (but the only one) in which I am inferior on the poll. The hot Dissenters here, and at Royston are numerous —But it will appear that throughout the county I have the *Quakers* strongly with me, though my anonymous libellers accuse me of inculcating *Perpetual War*. However, on the whole I made a better canvass at Hitchin that I expected, and even in this quarter, it afterwards appeared that some had been drawn off to me from the adverse party by the gentlemen who now represented the interest and family of the late Sir Thomas Salisbury (vizt. Mr. Burrows and Sir Robert Salisbury.) Sir J. Sebright, who had been indefatigable with Dorrien etc. in his own quarter and had afterwards been canvassing with Crawley in the neighbourhood of Luton, knowing I was at Hitchin, could not repress his zeal, but came over, and mounted on his horse in the Market Place, (it being Market Day) made a good popular harangue which was well received even in the heart of my enemies, and which had only one fault, that it was too complimentary to me. From Hitchin, H. Baker and I passed on the same day to Baldock, where we met Muthertie by appointment, the roads covered with frozen snow, the country we were to pass perfectly open, and, but for the circumstance of our horses being properly shod, extremely dangerous. Add to this a cutting wind from the east directly in our teeth. Baldock, with the assistance of Muthertie, Hindley Graves and Prior, was canvassed with the same success as Ware and Hertford. Thence, 6 miles to sleep at Julians—The same or worse roads, and the wind from the same quarter. An early breakfast at Julians enabled us to traverse in time the *Bay of Biscay*, which was one sheet of snow, to Ashwell where we had 19 out of 25 votes for us, of those whom we canvassed—here however several had been poisoned. From Ashwell, through the same country to Royston, where we were again in the enemy's country. It was Market Day—Brand there on his canvass—we met however with good humour on the Market Place, and afterwards at a private house to make some arrangements about the election. As our time was not likely to be profitably spent here, I proceeded with Muthertie to Newsells to pay our respects to Peachy. Barkway had been before canvassed in our favour, we called however on every freeholder there, and passed on to Buntingford where Dr. Wood received us, at dinner and for the evening. Thursday morning the 31st early we went round Buntingford where we had ¾ of the voters with us, from thence to Puckeridge, where it was necessary to call on 6 or 7. Here Muthertie left me, and I proceeded, through Standon (an enemy's country under the influence of Giles) to Stortford, where (it being Market Day) your Uncle Edward Leightenhouse and other zealous friends of the town, met me by appointment. We canvassed the place with much greater success than I had reason to expect—57 in my favour to 44 against me, and this, notwithstanding the numerous Dissenters in that quarter and the former prejudices about the Malt Tax, and the indirect use made by Halsey (Late Whately) of

Plumer's name in that and other quarters. On a subsequent report I found besides that several more promises had been given here in my favour, than I expected. In this part of my canvass I was particularly gratified, because it proved the people were really returned to a right sense of things. Sabridgeworth having been canvassed by Mrs. Milles's tenants, E. Conyers etc. to a man in my favour I reserved myself for a future day in paying my respects there, and reached home that evening. I had made an appointment with Dorrien, Sebright, Green etc. etc. to meet them on Friday morning the 1st instant at Gt. Berkhamsted by ten. My horses were sent on before, and I proceeded early to the place appointed—Gt. Berkhamsted North Church and Tring (Market Day at the last) were canvassed with the most decided success. Indeed our friends in this quarter had done wonders before my arrival. And at Tring in particular, Harding and Griffin carried all before them—so much so, that Halsey and Brand then on their canvass there, having not a man to speak to, shut themselves up in a public house, and on coming out to mount their horses were insulted by the populace with snow balls, which my friends . . . interfered to check. From Tring we passed up to our horses knees in snow cross the Earl of Bridgwater's country to Aldbury etc. by Gaddesden to Hemel Hempsted, which had been canvassed before by Sebright, Groves, Towers, Dorrien, etc. The success we had here was the more mortifying to Halsey as it is under his very nose at Gaddesden. Here, the ground being very slippery, I received a fall on my back which I felt the effects of for some days after. Beechwood was our head quarters for that evening— and a truly hospitable reception we met with—Sir John was now in his element—Zealous in the cause—personally attached to me, and delighted with the thing itself, as a bustling scene to which his talents are so peculiarly suited. Dorrien of the party, with equal steadiness and zeal, but in a more quiet way working with effect to the same object. An early breakfast on Saturday the 2nd enabled us to take Market Street, which had been secured to a man in my favour (and Redburn which had been partially so) in our way to St. Albans—not passing by Gorhambury, where notwithstanding former oppositions, I found Lord Grimston every thing I could wish—he had indeed expressed himself to that effect before in one of the handsomest letters ever written. St Albans was our grand object for this day —It was Market Day besides, and the utmost zeal prevailing there and in its neighbourhood, Sandridge Aldenham etc. It had been critically canvassed before—119 in my favour, 38 against, and 6 neuter—to these 119, 12 afterwards were added —5 had indeed taken a contrary direction, and of the 38 two proved afterwards neutrals and did not vote at all. This day was a very flattering one—I dined tête à tête with Lady Spencer and reached Bayford in the evening. Sunday the 3rd was dedicated as before to letters etc. etc. quiet and my family. Brand too called on me by appointment to make some arrangements about the day of election. He appeared far from sanguine, and evidently was forced on by his violent partizans without a chance of succeeding. We parted however, as before in perfect good humour. Monday the 4th was dedicated to Sir A. Hume who met me by appointment at Hoddesdon and we went through the whole of his district—well—Hoddesdon—Broxborne, Wormley, Cheshunt and Waltham Abbey—where we had 120 decidedly with us—and 7 only against. Returning home that evening I went down to Watford and Rickmansworth by appointment on Tuesday the 5th (Market Day) where under the wing of Lord Essex, Lord Clarendon and Mr. Williams of Moore Park, Mr. Salter and Mr. Clutterbuck we had a better division of interest than I expected, the enemy having made a partial impression in that quarter. However I had every reason to be satisfied Lord Essex received me at Cassiobury to dinner and to sleep ... Wednesday the 6th and all the morning of the 7th were passed in London, not inactively, as you may suppose—and I returned to a late dinner at Bayford on the latter day. The 8th (Friday morning) was dedicated by appointment to Sabridgeworth, where I met E. Conyers, the Mill having engaged me to breakfast at Pishio-

bury, and all the votes in their neighbourhood (between 50 and
60 having been engaged in my favour). This part of my progress
was therefore very flattering. Taking Thorley in my way, where
the zeal of my friends had secured all the votes (6 in number)
for me, I met Dr. Hamilton at the Hadhams, and had the same
flattering testimony in my favour (with a few exceptions) owing
to the activity of his family, the Gordons and John Calvert,
there and at Albury. The weather had now changed, and I
reached the Parsonage at Much Hadham (Dr. Hamilton's)
drenched to the skin. Here I dined and slept on the Friday . . .
After breakfast on Saturday the 9th I proceeded to Braughing,
where every thing had been done with great success for me by
Mr. Say the Clergyman, and the Priors, on the suggestion of
Mr. Houblon and Captain Harvey of Chigwell, both of whom
have estates in that quarter. The foxhounds had met that morning at Hammells and, as I might meet, as in fact I did, several
friends in the field, the occasion and the object together were
too tempting to be resisted, and accordingly, with the apothe-
cary of Puckeridge for my guide, we pushed on after the
hounds, found them running, killed our fox, shook several
friends by the hand at the death, and proceeded to Hertford,
where the carpenters, under the Market Place, in the erection
of the hustings, were giving dreadful sounds of preparation. The
remainder of Saturday could not be passed from home. It was
better employed in making preparation for breakfast at Bayford
and Hertingfordbury for such of the Freeholders, as coming
from the west and north chose to partake of refreshment, or
leave their horses. In this our farm was also included, with the
advantage of beds for many during the poll . . . The field was
very handsomely attended, and the business proceeded without
much delay, though greater than I could have wished. The
shew of flags in our favour from Stortford, Sabridgeworth, and
particularly from Sebright's quarter was splendid—and the
shew of carriages etc. striking. The scene, the sloping hill
above the Gaol. Sir John Sebright put me in nomination,
seconded by Sir Abraham Hume, our old friend Muthertie

giving the pas* to the 2 Baronets in the present instance. Hale proposed Brand and was seconded by Halsey. None of them were long. My Mover spirited, and to the purpose. Hale miserably faltering, he uttered one sentence with a tolerable memory, but forgot his lesson when he came to the second. Whitbread made a personal attack on me, which I repelled by a practical reproof as expressed in my Address, putting the Address itself into his hand, and desiring him to make the most of it, and point out, if he could, a syllable which would justify his assertions. This threw him all a-back—and a similar challenge to all the anonymous writers who had been pelting me during the canvass, gave me a decided advantage, not one of them daring to stand forth. Flower, contrary to his usual practice was tongue-tied. Giles, who was reported to have intended giving me a Philippic, was not there, and such had been the impression made on the minds of the Freeholders in general by Plumer's *professed* neutrality, and the scandalous manner in which Halsey had notwithstanding canvassed in his name, and this is not merely in that quarter of the county where his wife's estate lay, but in the very heart of Plumer's main strength, at Ware, Standon and Stortford (of which there were abundant proofs), that when Whitbread attempted a panegyric on Plumer in the course of his speech, describing him as their old, faithful and favourite candidate, the cry of the field was very general, and that among some of his best friends '*Aye! that WAS our favourite.*' Plumer himself, either to show his *neutrality*, or to avoid being catechised, was not there. But, besides these practices of Halsey, I am well assured that two houses in Eastwick were actually opened by *Mrs.* Plumer for Brand's voters. Can you then wonder that in my Address I should mark his conduct as mysterious and requiring explanation . . . The Sheriff declined the shew of hands in my favour—a poll was demanded for Brand and we proceeded from the field to the hustings. All the forenoon had been consumed in the field, and the poll did not commence till one or near one. On the close

* Precedence.

of the poll the first day the numbers were for me 861—for Brand 583. It was indeed evident from the beginning and through the whole canvass that I must succeed. The poll commenced at eight on the 2nd day (Tuesday the 12th) and it was agreed should finish for that day at 3. But more than half an hour before the time was expired—Brand declined, and on casting up the books, the numbers stood as in the enclosed card —for me 1556, for Brand 1076. The form of chairing round the town was carried into effect with much exultation on the part of my friends, and with perfect good humour on that of the enemy. Flower's wife was very ill in bed, and I had the opportunity of shewing a civility to him on the occasion by preventing the procession, and consequently the noise, being carried to that end of the town—and this, notwithstanding our hostility, was well received. Wilshere's coachman was the only outrageous character, as he had the insolence to drive his master's carriage full speed through the crowd at the time of chairing, to the risk of the lives of hundreds. Providentially, however, no person was materially injured. Brand made an apology to me afterwards by letter for the outrage, and Wilshere, though not at my desire, has since turned the servant away, as I only recommended an apology in the newspapers—should it appear that no one was hurt, and such legal prosecution, or other satisfaction to the parties injured, as Mr. W. should advise, in case any injury had been sustained.

You may well suppose that all this success has not been accomplished without much fatigue of body, great anxiety of mind, and that eventually will be attended with considerable expense. On the other hand the event has been to me, under all circumstances, peculiarly gratifying . . . Herts RO Baker MSS AR 354.

PART TWO

Borough Elections in England and Wales

INTRODUCTION

AT the general election of 1784, 215 English and Welsh boroughs returned 417 MPs to Wesminster; nineteen of these, including all twelve Welsh boroughs, being single-member constituencies. By 1830 there were one borough and two members fewer, and the parliamentary reformers were arguing that, taken as a whole, the borough members had little claim to represent the social and economic interests of the towns and cities of England and Wales. They were, of course, correct. To quote just one of their main arguments: over half the English borough members were returned for constituencies in the arc of southern counties along the coastline from the Wash to the Severn, a reflection of the days when the commercial strength of the country was in the south of England, as opposed to the Midlands and the North. Furthermore, there was no uniform borough franchise in the boroughs as there was in the counties, which meant that, at best, different social groups were represented haphazardly or, at worst, not at all. There were in fact seven groups of boroughs, each distinguished by a particular franchise:

(i) 101 'freeman' boroughs, in which the right to vote belonged to the freemen of the corporation, a status usually gained by inheritance (birth, redemption and marriage) or service (apprenticeship to a trade), although there was a long history in some boroughs of 'honorary' freemen appearing in strength before and during an election. Taken together they possessed some distinctive characteristics. Contested elections were often dominated by a conflict between the corporation itself and interests amongst the freemen, many of whom, in the larger constituencies, were men of little or no property. It was often the case that these contests were between an Anglican-dominated corporation and nonconformist interests amongst the freemen, or between economic interests that were to some extent reflected in those religious differences. Another characteristic, and one that became increasingly important as the period progressed, was that varieties of urban radicalism were more effective in constituencies of this type than in others.

(ii) Thirty-six 'scot and lot' boroughs, where the vote belonged to the independent householders who paid the poor rate—a qualification that excluded the poorer sections of the constituency. Unfortunately they defy generalisation as a few, like Westminster, had large electorates in which a variety of interests were in conflict, while others were small enough to be prey to patronage and management. The majority of 'scot and lot' electorates, however, were sizeable enough to attract competing proprietary interests and this led to bitter and expensive contests.

(iii) Twenty-nine 'burgage' boroughs, where the vote was attached to property—usually a house and a small amount of land—with the result that elections were solely determined by those who owned the burgages.

(iv) Twenty-eight 'corporation' boroughs, where only members of the corporation could vote. Here electorates were small, and elections could turn on the social and economic standing of the members of the corporation. If they were chiefly small merchants and traders, they easily succumbed to the influence of the neighbouring gentry; if they were men of substance and independence, they decided the outcome amongst themselves.

(v) Twelve 'householder' or 'potwalloper' boroughs, in which the vote belonged to all inhabitant householders. These boroughs possessed the most unlimited franchise of all; yet ironically their elections were determined largely by the most flagrant exercise of bribery, and least of all by political considerations.

(vi) Six 'freeholder' boroughs, where freeholders with 40s or more of freehold property possessed the vote.

(vii) One borough, in which the freeholders, freemen and the inhabitant householders all voted.

The total borough electorate in 1784 was approximately 110,000, and in 1830 nearly 190,000.

The interests of those towns and cities that were represented were therefore reflected through a kaleidoscope, with, as an example, large towns suffering a very restricted franchise, and other small and insignificant ones enjoying almost complete male suffrage. Yet by placing too much emphasis upon the distinctive characteristics that developed from a particular franchise, it is possible to obscure those features common to borough politics: features concerning those who normally controlled borough elections and the methods they employed, the attitudes of voters, electoral practices, and the character of political activity. It is these features which can provide a particular focus for our attention, and which have, for that reason, been selected for illustration in the documents and for further discussion.

Although the property qualification for a borough MP of £300 of freehold land was less than that for a county member, the landed classes still largely prevailed in borough elections. The weight of property adjacent to or in a borough was often sufficient to put it into the owner's pocket, or at least bring it under his patronage or management. Furthermore, the lack of elbow room in county elections often obliged landed gentlemen to seek an outlet in the boroughs. Business and professional men, on the other hand, who wanted to found an electoral interest often took a considerable risk; and one that newly acquired capital might be unable to bear. It was, after all, cheaper and of less risk to buy a seat from a patron, a common practice which largely accounts for the relatively high number of borough MPs drawn from outside the landed classes. Proprietorial interests were therefore a vital factor in borough elections. In some cases, as in the 'burgage' borough of Old Sarum (28), where property itself was enfranchised, they were decisive; but in most boroughs a mixture of influence and artful persuasion, which could work to the advantage of both the patron and the inhabitants of the borough, was applied. Of the seventeen members of the Helston corporation who possessed the vote only two were in any sense dependent upon the patron, the Duke of Leeds, whose influence clearly depended upon his benefactions in the borough (29). In the freeman boroughs of York and Grimsby (30, 31), the interests of Earl Fitzwilliam and George Tennyson required careful and thoughtful management; and even in the case of the 'close' borough of Fowey (32) it is easy to see how the economic life of the borough was closely connected with electoral considerations. In some respects, therefore, proprietorial interests in the boroughs could resemble those in the counties. Success with them depended upon careful management and attention to the needs of those who came within their orbit. Thomas Lennard's charitable contributions when MP for Ipswich (33) are an example of this near paternal situation.

The main opposition to established proprietary interests, in those constituencies where they predominated, came from landlords who themselves wished to become established and who were usually bound to exercise the same influence as their opponents. However, opposition from social and economic interests outside the landed classes was relatively frequent, although it was not of such a uniform character as that in the counties. William Bartindale's forthright independence was a factor that the Earl Fitzwilliam had to conjure with in Malton in 1807 (34); while the 1789 handbill attacking Edward Lovedon's contribution to the economic wellbeing of Abingdon (35) expressed a general complaint that was of a kind often made during this period. However, it was perhaps in the freemen boroughs that opposition to established interests took its most coherent form. In Derby in 1823, for example, the corporation was not too happy with the services of their MPs who stood on the interests of the Duke of Devonshire (36); and in Carlisle in 1816 the freemen were expressing their disgruntlement with the influence of the corporation (37).

In terms of procedure, borough elections were similar to those in the counties although in practice there were significant differences. There was, for example, a much larger proportion of uncontested returns due to the large number of close boroughs. The account of the election for Marlborough in 1790 is an excellent example of an uncontested return for a 'close' borough (38). Furthermore, when contested elections did take place, venality, rowdyism and sharp practice played a much more significant part in the smaller electorates of the boroughs than they did in the counties. The examples of the turbulence at the Durham election of 1802 (39) and the Westminster, Liverpool and Leicester elections (46–9) are interesting in this respect; while the extract from the annotated Leominster poll-book demonstrates a kind of corruption impossible to manage in a county election (40).

There were also differences in other respects. As has already been indicated in the discussion of county elections, landlords found it difficult to coerce voters within their interests into voting as they wished. However, in those boroughs where pro-prietorial interests depended upon a tenant vote as in the 'scot and lot' boroughs, smaller electorates and less secure tenures made this possible. The summary of the Newark pollbook illustrates the sway of the landlords there (41), and it is significant that the thinnish support given to Earl Fitzwilliam by his tenants in Malton in 1807 (42) led him to turn out those who had failed to toe the line. The Duke of Newcastle followed Fitzwilliam's example at Newark in 1831 (43). In other words, while most borough interests were based upon an acceptance of mutual obligations, some were despotic in character.

Yet the most significant difference of all lay in the scope that the larger boroughs provided for the debate of what were purely political issues. In the counties the influence of property was so strong, and the social strata from which the voters were drawn so narrow, that political issues tended to be of low significance. In the larger boroughs, particularly the larger freemen boroughs, electorates could often encompass a range of social interests and at the same time be beyond the range of traditional means of influence. In such constituencies more efficient techniques of electoral management were developed, and national and provincial politics swam to the surface. At Westminster in 1818, for example, the radical interest was organised upon an almost modern basis (48), while at Leicester in 1826 the Catholic and Corn Law questions played a role in deciding the outcome of the election (49). Of course, the number of constituencies in which political issues were of major importance was small— perhaps no more than twenty—yet they were the constituencies which the reformers looked to with enthusiasm and which pointed the way to the future.

Section one: AN EXAMPLE OF A ROTTEN BOROUGH
28 Old Sarum, Wiltshire, 1802-3
The franchise belonged to the burgage holders. In June 1802, Lord Camelford sold the borough to the Earl of Caledon for £43,000. The following document shows the situation under Lord Camelford; the names in brackets are those of the new voters that Caledon created by leases executed in May 1803.

A List of the Burgage Tenures in Old Sarum belonging to the Right Honourable Thomas Lord Camelford

No.	Tenements	Quantity			Freeholders for Life—Voters	Occupiers
	On the South Side of the Portway	A	r	P		
1	Jerseys	5	1		Revᵈ Thoˢ Burrough, of Abbots Ann [Richard Dann]	Mʳ John Whitchurch
2	Blundel's Garden or Hart's Close	7	3	20	Revᵈ Jnᵒ Skinner DD of New Sarum [James Law, 18 Portland Place, London]	Mʳ John Phelps Geary

No.	Tenements	Quantity			Freeholders for Life—Voters	Occupiers
	On the South Side of the Portway	*A*	*r*	*P*		
3	Phillips's two Acres	1	3	24	---------------- [Langford Heyland, Glen Oak, Co. Antrim]	Mᵣ John Whitchurch
4	Harvey of Chigwell's eight Acres	6	3	8	Joseph Massey Stratford [James Du Pré, 3 Grafton Street, Dublin]	Mᵣ John Whitchurch
5	Turvill's two Acres	1	3	12	---------------- [Henry Alexander, 13 Queen St., Westminster]	Dᵒ
6	The Farm-three Acres	2	2	38	---------------- [Robert Alexander, 7 Sackville St., Dublin]	Dᵒ
	On the North Side of the Portway					
7	Elliot's late Franklins	0	1	9	Wᵐ Dyke Esqᵣ Syren Cot near Sarum [Thomas Redhead, Nottingham Place, London]	Joseph Massey
8	Rosewells late Wyndhams	0	3	8	William Dean, Wimborne [William Dean]	Joseph Brunsdon
9	Elliot's (the electing acre)	0	2	16	Joseph Brunsdon of Stratford [Joseph Brunsdon]	Dᵒ
10	Harveys Little Croft	1	3	27	Revᵈ Benjⁿ Forster of Bocconnoc [William Alexander Jnr.]	John Whitchurch
11	Greens late Cooper's	1		16	---------------- [Henry Redhead, 57 Devonshire St., London]	Dᵒ

N.B. The pieces of Land of which the Quantities are given above are understood to be the land to which the right of voting is particularly attached altho' many of them are parts— only of Tenements consisting some of Houses & Lands, and some of other lands with! houses—as may be seen by the description of some of the Tenements. The whole Tenement is in many instances granted to the Voters, as supposed out of Caution.

The several Tenements against which no Names of Lifeholders appear are vacant; Nᵒ 3 became so on the death of the Revᵈ John Burrough—Nᵒ 5 on the death of the late Mᵣ Portman and Nᵒ 6 on the death of Lieut. Genᵉ Cowper — Elliotts (the electing Acre). N°. 9 is considered as the absolute Property of Joseph Brunsdon an old Carpenter at Stratford for his life—the late Lord Camelford having directed that he should pay no Rent for it. They are all granted by Lease & Release to the respective Voters for their natural lives, without any reservation of Rent. Rosewell's (N°. 8) is held under Lord Camelford by Lease for 99 years determinable on 3 lives. PRO NI, Caledon MSS, TD 2282/7.

Section two: ELECTIONS IN SOME MIDDLE-SIZED CONSTITUENCIES: MARKET AND COUNTY TOWNS WITH A VARIETY OF DIFFERENT FRANCHISES

29 The state of Helston, Cornwall, in 1802

Pop c 2,200 and a corporation electorate of seventeen. The strongest interest was that of George Godolphin, 6th Duke of Leeds, for whom this report was written.

Report respecting the Borough of Helston [20 Oct. 1802]

Before the present state of it is described, it may be proper to give a short sketch of it's History.

The Corporation of Helston, by the original Charter granted in the 27th year of Queen Eliz. & confirmed by a subsequent Charter of Charles the 1st, was to consist of a Mayor 4 Aldermen & an indefinite number of Freemen, in whom the Right of Election of Burgesses to serve in Parliament was vested.

In 1773 the Corporation consisted of only one Alderman & 7 Freemen—on which account it was alledged that it could no longer continue itself.

In September 1774 a new Charter was granted, by which 5 Aldermen (one to be Mayor) and 31 Freemen were appointed, and which included the single Alderman & 7 Freemen of the old Body—6 of the old Corporators protested against the new Charter—but the rest who were named, accepted it. Soon afterwards, there was an Election for Members to serve in Parliament. The Mayor and Corporators who had accepted the new Charter elected the Marquis of Carmarthen & Fran.

Owen Esqr. and the old Corporators elected Philip Yorke & Fran. Cust Esqrs., who petitioned the House of Commons against the return of the former, and the Committee decided that the Petitioners were duly elected, thereby confirming the old Charter.

At the general election in 1790, the same contest for the election of members was renewed, when the Mayor and Corporators under the new Charter elected & returned Sir Gilbert Elliot & Sir Stephen Lushington; and Richard Bonhall (the only existing Corporator under the old Charter) elected & returned J. Bland Burges & Chas. Abbott Esqr. This double Return was heard before a Committee of the House of Commons, who then decided in favour of the new Charter. The Court of Kings Bench having in the period between those two opposite decisions, determined the right to be in the Corporators under the new Charter—that Right seems now to be so fixed.

By the new Charter, the Mayor, or his Deputy and Aldermen or major part of them (the Mayor or his Deputy to be one) are annually to meet on the Sunday next before Michaelmas Day, & nominate 2 of the Aldermen before the Freemen then present, that one of the two may be elected Mayor who, in case of sickness or absence may appoint a Deputy. And, in all corporate Acts, the Mayor or his Deputy (if the Votes are equal) has a double, or casting Vote.

Present state of the Borough [and electorate of Helston]

[20 Oct. 1802]

which consists of a Mayor, 4 Aldermen & 12 Freemen only—viz.

Mr. John Rowe (Mayor) – aged abt. 68 – His Grace's [The Duke of Leeds'] Agent—in property independent.

John Rogers Esqr.   – about 50   – heretofore one of the Members for Helston, where he has considerable property—has not lately intermeddled much with the affairs of the Corporation

		—but supposed not friendly to the Duke's interest.
Revd. John Passmore	– about 50	– possesses the living of St. Just —said to have been procured thro' the Interest of the Duke's family—claims a promise of additional preferment from his grace.
Revd. Richd. Grylls	– about 45	– possesses a good living from his own family besides a paternal estate.—but solicits and expects another living from his Grace's patronage— he has great influence in the Borough.
Mr. Thos. Grylls	– about 42	– Brother to the last—a solicitor of eminence—has acquired an independent fortune. It is supposed the 2 brothers can command a Majority of Influence in the Corporation.
Thos. Moore	– about 80	– nearly superannuated— independent in circumstances.
John Tremayne	– about 77	– a Surgeon—supposed to be needy.
Richard Johns	– about 71	– was a solicitor—but has declined the profession, & is independent.
Wm. Skuds	– about 63	– holds an office in the Duchy under the Prince of Wales.
Revd. Thos. Trevathan	– abt. 57	– holds the united livings of Shobbear & Sheepwash in Devonshire.
John Harris	– about 56	– resides at Polwyn, upon his own estate.
Isaac Hoad	– about 50	– a respectable surgeon in Helston.
John Trevenen Esqr.	– abt. 46	– has a large estate at Bonithon (near Helston) where he resides.
Peter Hill	– about 44	– an independent Gentleman in Helston.

John Johns	– about 44	– Do.—he is a son of Richard Johns.
Revd. Thos. Robinson	– about 42	– resides at Helston—has a small living—expects the Duke to get him a better.
Revd. Wm. Tremayne	– about 40	– appointed by the Duke to do duty at the Scilly Isles—worth about £80 a year.—His conduct is stated to be strange, & often irregular.

Remarks

His Grace's property at Helston is but small—and from its nature (being generally granted out on leases for lives which are occasionally renewed) attaches no kind of influence over the Borough. The Godolphin Interest (as it has been called) appears to have been kept up at a monstrous expence, not only by erecting repairing, & ornamenting public buildings belonging to the Borough, but by liberal and sometimes extravagant provisions made for, and by patronage exerted on behalf of those individual members of it, who possessed the greatest influence in the Corporation; and also by public entertainments to the Corporators—and (what is worst of all) by the constant and uniform payment (whenever that interest is allowed to prevail) of all the poor and Church Rates belonging to the whole Borough, which will now amount (communibus annis) to 7 or £800 a year—and in the late years of scarcity to above £1000. This burthen (which the Corporators admit, but will not consent to remove) is the more vexatious, by reason that the estates of numbers of persons (possessing great property within the Borough, but who are no part of the Body Corporate) are wholly exonorated from those Taxes. Exclusive of those heavy charges, the Duke has frequent calls from the Corporators for patronage and provision for themselves & Friends, which must be attended to or his interest is diminished. And, after all, it appears to the Reporter, his Grace's influence in the Borough is of so precarious a nature, that he may continue these ex-

pences, & the exertion of his patronage on behalf of the Corporators, to the very Eve of another Election; and that even
then, he may not be able to secure the Return of a single
Member.

BM Add. MSS 33110 ff. 48–9.

J.B. Octr. 20th, 1802.

---

30 Preparations for an election. York, 1789

Pop c 16,000 and a freeman electorate of c 2,500. At the
1784 election, the interest which had commanded the return
for some time—that of Earl Fitzwilliam's family—was
defeated by a combination of the strengths of the Yorkshire
Association and the independent spirit in the city, the new
members being Lord Galway and Richard Milnes. The
Fitzwilliam party were determined to recapture at least one
seat, and in this letter Sinclair discusses ways of doing this
for their candidate, Sir William Milner. At the election in
1790, Sinclair's hopes were only partially fulfilled: Milner
was returned but the other seat was taken by Richard
Milnes.

Robert Sinclair to Lord Fitzwilliam

19 April 1789

I have not for a moment forgot the purport of your last letter,
but from the hurry of the circuit and other reasons have not
hitherto been able to give it an answer to my satisfaction. On
Friday last I got together Carr, Hartley, Wilson and Ellis—and
submitted to their joint consideration, the question of aiming
at the whole of the representation of this place. The opinion of
the majority (in which Carr and Hartley were included) was
that as things in general now stand, we are sure of Sir William
Milner—that in case a compromise should be offered to us we
ought to accede to it—that if we were, at present, to refuse such
an offer, Sir William might be in danger—that if our enemies
were to attempt to bring forward a joint candidate with Milnes,

we may with great hopes of success oppose with Sir William and his friend—that the party which *first* offers to aim at getting two members, will run great risk of absolute defeat—and that in case we can make up our minds to be satisfied with Sir William only, we may safely leave things as they now are without much additional trouble or expense before the actual commencement of the canvass. Such, I give you, as the sentiments of the majority of the meeting. And so I deemed it incumbent upon me to do clearly and explicitly. If however you think proper to attend to it seriously, I should willingly lay before you also the thoughts of some of the individuals present. It was by them alleged that with the assistance of Lord Hawke and Lord Galway, and in favour of a man of weight and character in the town, and also with the judicious expenditure of a little money by way of preparation, we might safely attempt to bring in a friend with Sir William—not by immediately avowing it, but gradually and imperceptibly or cautiously laying the foundation of such avowal; that circumstances were much changed since the last election; several of our most violent enemies were either dead, bankrupt, or otherwise silenced; that our party was a fixed phalanx; that some of the better sort of people had come over to us; that experiments have been lately made of forming some of the lower people into Clubs with an active friend or two of ours at the heads of them and giving such Clubs on the evenings of meeting two or three guineas to spend and thus wheedling in by art a few of the adherents of our enemies; that we had already paid for the expense of taking up freedoms for about 130 whom we have reason to think will be firm for us, whilst the other party have not got the length of 20 or 25; that by extending these schemes and plans, particularly as to the formation and encouragement of Clubs, a few months might do wonders—etc. etc. Such were the arguments of some of the gentlemen present.

Upon the evening of the late illuminations here I took the liberty of sending, at your Lordship's expense, 2 or 3 guineas a-piece to a number of the lower alehouses in remote corners of the town, with directions to have a few of their neighbours to drink with them to the King's health etc. This gave rise to the establishment of two or three monthly Clubs of freemen, which I have got one or two better sort of shopkeepers etc. to attend, and lay down upon the occasion a guinea or two upon the credit of the party, and I have already seen some very good effects from these little schemes—and I am strongly inclined to think that perseverance and a moderate extension of such a system would, with the expenditure [of] a very few hundred pounds, in three or four months work powerfully into the interest of our antagonists, and might in that time, have effects which few people at present can foresee. These I mention to your Lordship as my own private sentiments as well as those of one individual whose acquaintance amongst the lower people is greatly more extended than mine and of whose opinion in matters of this kind I have reason to think with respect. His name is Ellis, and he has, himself a number of persons constantly employed in his business. If your Lordship should deem it an object to carry two members such I conceive would be best mode of preparation for it, besides, authorising half a dozen of your friends here to employ agents to look after the out-voters in like manner. In a word the expense of ensuring Sir William, we all think, will be little or nothing in addition to what we have already laid out. That of opening further and prosecuting the plan above hinted with a more extended view, must be something more although I am told it need not be considerable.

I have been informed with some appearance of credit that Milnes himself is very anxious for a compromise but that Burgh and Mr. Wilberforce are decidedly against it. If they should take any steps indicative of war you may be assured we shall take the alarm and do what we can to counteract them. In the meantime until we know your further sentiments we shall endeavour to keep our present ground—I mean to give Sir William a line or two by this post, with whom I should wish your Lordship to confer a little, and to give me your ideas

upon the matter. Sheffield City Library, Wentworth Woodhouse Muniments, F 115/1.   ———

31 Strengthening an interest. Great Grimsby, 1818–19
Pop c 1,500 and a freeman electorate of c 300. Both Lord
Yarboro' and the Tennysons had strong interests in a borough
which was 'second to none in the history of corruption'.
Charles Tennyson was first returned in 1818 and after his
election presented a bottle of wine to each of the fathers of
ninety-two children due to be christened.

———

George Oliver to George Tennyson   24 Nov. 1818, Grimsby
If I might presume to give my opinion as to the probable
means of increasing your interest, I should advise you to *build*
upon every vacant spot of ground you are possessed of, which
is well situated for that purpose. Thus you would give employment to a great number of freemen; remunerate Mr. Joys (who
is a phalanx of strength in election matters) for the injuries
which it is said are doing to him from *another quarter*; and gain
also a greater number of permanent tenants, and consequently
friends to your cause; for tho' Cook has deceived you, I can
by no means think that his conduct would be general. Let Mr.
Heneage's estates be divided into fields of four or six acres; and
let these, together with your own estates be placed in the hands
of freemen to whom they would be *an object of importance*. Provide, if possible, small farms for the *sons* of Lord Yarbro's
tenants; and by these united means you will break into his
Lordship's interest, gain a decided superiority at present, and
secure the next generation almost entirely to yourself.

———

Later—in 1819—the port's tide surveyor decided to retire
and John Lusby informed Tennyson's son, Charles, of the
electioneering value of the post.

———

John Lusby to Charles Tennyson   11 May 1819
The fixed salary is £100 p. annum besides occasional per-
quisites amounting to about £20 but the patronage it produces

in the Borough is everything i.e. the employment of extra men 2 to every ship by this officer, and those men selected from *what party* amongst the unemployed freemen or others *he pleases* may ensure the certain support of not less than 10 to 15 at present to the interest he may be attached, and so in proportion as trade increases; you will therefore see the necessity of *immediately* applying to have the nomination in *yourself*. Grimsby Public Library, Tennyson Papers.

32 A borough agreement. Fowey, Cornwall, 1819

Pop c 1,500 and a 'scot and lot' electorate of c 250. In 1818, William Rashleigh, whose family had controlled at least one seat since 1798, sold his Fowey property to George Lucy, of Warwickshire. Lucy then entered into this agreement with Joseph Austen, who owned the most property in the borough. The agreement was witnessed by Lord Mount Edgcumbe, who also had a powerful interest.

Agreement between Lucy and Austen   20 July 1819

The Principle of this Agreement is that Mr. Lucy and his heirs are to have the Nomination of one Candidate and Mr. Austen and his heirs of the other.

That on the first Vacancy of either of the present Members Mr. Lucy is to have the sole Nomination, and that the successive Vacancies of one Member shall be filled up by the Interest making the Vacancy, that is, if the second Vacancy is occasioned on the Part and Interest of Mr. Austen, Mr. Austen is to have the second Nomination, and so on future Vacancies.

That at a general Eelection one Candidate shall be named on the part of Mr. Lucy and one on the Part of Mr. Austen.

That previous to a General Election it shall be decided by agreement or by Lot that if one Member only shall be returned by the joint Interest, which of the two Candidates shall be so returned and if only one is returned the Nomination on the next Vacancy shall belong to that Party who had not the preceding Nomination.

That a Lease is to be granted of Mr. Lucy's Houses and lands
in the Borough and Parish of Fowey and of such Right as he
may have in the Markets and Fairs of the same Borough to Mr.
Austen for seven years at a Rent or Rents to be ascertained in the
Schedule to such Lease, Mr. Lucy to have the Power of determining that Lease on giving six Months Notice at any period of
the year. The Lease to be void on the death of Mr. Austen.

Mr. Lucy engages if this agreement is fulfilled by Mr. Austen
to renew the Lease for successive Periods of seven years (with
the like Provision of determining it) if Mr. Austen shall so long
live, at such Rent as may then be agreed upon.

Mr. Lucy engages to make all his Burgage Tenants as available as he can and so as best to further the united Interest.

Mr. Austen engages not to agitate whilst Lessee any Question
respecting the Rights of the Tenants of his Manor of Fowey to
be admitted Tenants upon the Rolls of the Court of the Borough
and Manor of Fowey without Prejudice to Mr. Austen's Rights
of Suspension.

Both Parties engage not to erect such Houses or Buildings
except on Sites already built upon unless by mutual Consent.

All Indictments, Actions and other Suits at Law to be dis-
continued and quashed on both sides except such as Both
Parties shall agree to continue; And no new Prosecution or
Actions to be commenced except both Parties agree by which
is meant chiefly such Actions of Ejectment as it may be proper
to bring for the support of the united interest.

Mr. Austen is not to have the Power of granting under leases
of any part of the Property to be leased to him by Mr. Lucy,
but the Occupiers are to be Tenants at will.

Up to this Time each Party to pay his own Costs of all Law
Proceedings.

That the Expences of any legal Proceedings hereafter to be
instituted by the Consent of Both Parties or against the united
Interest to be borne at the joint Expence. Mr. Lucy to have the
Conduct of such Suits as affect his Property and Mr. Austen of
those which affect his.

That the Expences of future Elections are thus to be defrayed —If an Election of one Member takes place the Expences to be defrayed by the Candidate or the Person on whose Interest he stands. If a general Election the expences to be defrayed by both Parties equally.

It is understood that nothing herein contained is to extend to prevent the Earl of Mount Edgcumbe from taking any Measures that may be thought advisable to obtain a Modification of the present Charter.

If any Differences or Disputes should arise between Mr. Lucy and Mr. Austen either respecting the true [intent] of this Agreement or the Propriety of pursuing any Measures with respect to the Borough or any other ground or Occasion such Matters so in dispute shall be referred to the decision of two Arbitrators to be chosen by each Party, and they to name an Umpire if necessary.

To these Heads of Agreement Mr. Lucy and Mr. Austen declare upon their Honours they will agree and strictly perform to the utmost of their Power, Witness their Hands this twentieth Day of July 1819.

Witness   R. G. Macdonald.   *George Lucy.*
                                              Josh. Thos. Austen.

And the Earl of Mount Edgcumbe & Viscount Valletort hereby testify their Approbation of this Agreement and engage upon their Honour to endeavour as far as may be in their Power to support the same on all Occasions.

                                                   Valletort

Treffrey Papers

---

33 Charities to which a member for Ipswich contributed, 1821–6

Pop c 17,000 and a freeman electorate of c 750. A venal borough in which the Crickett banking family had the strongest personal interest. Lennard was elected on petition in 1820 but did not contest the borough in 1826.

Thomas Barrett Lennard's account with Mr. Pearson

1821   Dr. to William Pearson

		£	s	d
Oct. 5	To acct. then delivered	56	11	6
	Paid Thos. Bevan of Stonham Pie when you went to the Fox dinner for change of silver	1	0	0
	By half subscription to the Members' Plate at the races from 1820 to 1825 both inclusive, the whole subscription being £21 a year and which was equally divided between you and Wm. Haldimand Esq.	63	0	0
	By half donation to the ringers at £8 8s. a year from 1821 to 1825 which was likewise divided between you and Mr. Haldimand	16	16	0
	The Xmas Box to the Town Servants from 1821 to 1825 at £4 4s. a year which was likewise divided between you and Mr. Haldimand	8	8	0
	By half donation to the Town Band at £2 2s. per annum from 1820 to 1825 which was likewise divided	5	5	0
	By subscription to the Ipswich Lying In Charity from 1820 to 1826 at £1 6s. per annum including 5s. entrance	8	1	0
	By subscription to the Ipswich Female benefit Society from 1820 to 1826 at £1 1s. per annum	6	6	0
	By ditto to the Ipswich Education Society from 1821 to 1826 at £1 1s. per annum	5	5	0
	By ditto to the Red Sleeve Charity School from 1821 to 1826 at £1 1s. p.a.	5	5	0
	By ditto to the Charity for the Relief of the Widows and Orphans of the Clergy from 1821 to 1826 at £1 1s. p.a.	5	5	0
	By subscription to the Friendly Society from 1820 to 1826 at £1 6s. p.a.	7	16	0
	By ditto to Lancastrian School from 1820 to 1826 at £1 1s. p.a.	6	6	0
	By ditto to the Mendicity Society from 1820 to 1826 at 16s. p.a.	4	16	0
1824				
July 4	Paid at your request when you were present for a treat to the Freemen at the Admiral's Head	5	5	0

1823			£	s	d
July	3	Paid for 12 Box Tickets for the theatre this evening you having bespoken the play at the request of the Manager	2	8	0
July	5	Paid Thomas Alderton for repairing your carriage		5	0
1821					
July	28	Paid Messrs. King and Garrod for printing 500 reports of your speech on the Alien Bill for the Freemen	8	0	0
			215	18	6
July	30	Paid half advertising Public Dinner to celebrate the return of you and Mr. Haldimand		10	6
1826					
May	6	Paid advertising your address to the Ipswich Freemen stating your intention to withdraw yourself from the Borough	2	2	0
			218	11	0

Essex RO D/DL 041/3

34 A voter explains his thoughts about the Malton election of 1807

Malton, Yorks, 1807; pop c 3,000 and a 'scot and lot' electorate of c 500. Earl Fitzwilliam possessed the strongest interest and in 1807 supported the candidacy of Major Robert Laurence Dundas and Bryan Cooke against that of Isaac Leatham, a local landowner, and Lord Headley. Dundas and Headley were returned but unseated on petition. Cooke won the ensuing by-election in 1808. The Mr Hastings in the following letter was a Fitzwilliam agent.

William Bartindale to Lord Fitzwilliam
Malton, 26 October 1807

My Lord,

I make bold to rite to you, and as your lordship may belave me I would be sorry to be impartenent to you, and as the truthe & the intention I hev in riting will be in your lordships poor to

D

prove or disprove by enquiries, I hop my liberty will be ekskusd and my motive be weel takken.

Noo if your lordship will be so gud as to enquir aboot what I say, youl find, at there isnt a Gentlemen in allt Neyburhud at all beloov'd eksept Mr. leatham, but hated, I meen among the lower & middlin glas of Borgesses and freehods, there must consekwently be sum reason for lord Headley gettin in, and that was pately on accoont or his beginin before Mr. leatham, bud cheefly on accoont of Hastin's behavier—for he was so mich dislikd at people wer intarmend to seport fost et com, whoever it was, and its my opinion, your lordship may pleas yourself, bud you may threaten, & discharge as you will, but youl nivver get mare an one member for Malton if Hastings is to paddigoad and strut over us this is my opinion, and ahve livd longer in Malton than him—this your lordship may depend ont is the Kease, whatever you may conclewd from letters ritten in fear & thro selfishness, tit contrary. I myself hev a close of yours, but, not to offend, bud to convince you, I shall give it up on leady day nekst without repahnin. Ahve, thenk God, an independence suffishent for me, and can onny day muster 20 Votes. Ah nivver should hev acted as I did, oot of resentment to your lordship. The Rockingham blood I alway's lik'd. The Bartindales is one of the oldest faimles in the Boro—but ahve been injur'd oot of boonds by this man—cumplaints hev been often maid by several bud withoot onny effect—map's they nivver reachd your lorship—didnt he, in my absence, go to my poor old Mother, frighten her oot of a key, enter a Malt Kill & primisis, built by my Uncle, which as I follow'd Maltin was worth £150 a year to me, withoot previous notis, & let it to other people. When I bote my freehods the frutes of monny years care & industry did he not commence an action to rob me of certain rites in it—and when he was bet & when of corse your lordship was to pay all expences amoontin to 23 or 25£ did he not get to my Attorney, one of those Rascals he keeps in his interest by rent dinners &c & tamper with him so that I had to pay costs myself—did he not bring an action of ejectment against me for some land I had under your lordship, withoot previous notis and force me into £10 or thereaboot ekspenses, or I should have lost £50. Tho this, maps, may be y'an of the worst Keases, yet on *proper* enkuiry, mind I say proper enkwiry, youl find his general behaver tendin to this. he has robb'd, & plunder'd, & harrasd several in this way. Did your lordship ivver hear of his roboin the Cow Paster of a stack of hay which he sold for above £30, and that wh[en] the poor beasts were put to the Paster there was no [fora]ge for them. Noo, for my own part my lord whar was there to bind me to your interest. Right glad should I be for my own pate, to see things as they wer, and a sensibl clever fellow, would in my opinion bring it aboot shortly—Hastings you may depend on it nivver will—he begins to be more insultin an ivver. When it was ekspected the event of the Malton election would hev kick'd him oot, it is found he holds his hod, & the blew freehods are bitterer at the heart an ivver. Ahl giv your lordship a sample of his prisent behaver. The other day I was on the jury at Old Malton—two of us had voted against your lordship Us two he left out and took the rest to dine with him in corse us two were obliged to tak his leavins. And this he did to a Malton bargess—who can thro into the scale 20 votes. this cartenly isnt calcalated to tiee you over. Noo, my lord as a prove that I didnt feel resentment towards your lordship I went, on foot with 5 plumpers [voters intending to cast single votes], at my own ekspense to vote for my lord Milton—I dont suppose at actions like these, many such heving been perform'd by the independent Borgesses, hev been mention'd to your lordship. For my bit of a close my lord I don't care a fig—tho you may depend on my future seport if Hastings is walk'd hoff, or chang'd considerably in his behaver. of the truth of what ahve sed ahve a bundl of proofs I trust your lordship will do what is best am your obdt servant etc. Sheffield City Library, Wentworth Woodhouse Muniments, f 76/118.

———

35 An anonymous handbill designed to undermine the position of the member for Abingdon, 1789

Pop c 4,000 and a 'scot and lot' electorate of c 240. Edward Loveden was elected for this single member constituency in 1783 and continued to represent it until 1796. He owned considerable property near the borough, but it was calculated that about half the electorate was influenced by the corporation, about seventy took money and that the Dissenters had strong interests too.

Handbill, to E. L. Loveden, Esq., Member for the Borough of Abingdon, Berks.

Sir,

As you have not thought proper to answer the letter addressed to you in the London Evening Post, of the 28th of March ultimo, I take the liberty of proposing a few Queries to you, having been furnished with some materials for the occasion by a friend who is pretty conversant in the local politics of the town of Abingdon.

Was you not obtruded on the borough of Abingdon by two of the Corporation servants in the night time, and before the rest of the inhabitants were acquainted with the loss which they and the country had sustained by the unfortunate death of their truly worthy Member, Mr. Howarth?

Did not the Electors suppress their indignation against those officious persons, and generously and independently elect you, without fee or reward, in full expectation that your conduct would have corresponded with your loyal and constitutional professions?

Did you not reprobate, in the strongest terms, the coalition of North, Fox, and Burke, and pledge yourself to support Mr. Pitt in his constitutional endeavours to rescue your King and Country from the tyranny of that mischievous and nefarious junto?

Did you not cause foxes and other vermin to be exhibited on a gallows, for the derision of the populace, and then consigned them to the flames, declaring 'they were types of what the Coalition ought to be?'

Did you not acquiesce in a most destructive Canal scheme, calculated to annihilate a great part of the trade of that borough which it was your particular duty to protect, and because you expected to make at least 25 per cent profit on a large capital you had subscribed, that your income might be at least equal to that of a little Lord?

Did you not cajole some of your constituents, by gilding the bitter pill you was preparing for them to swallow, by permitting them, (as a matter of great favour), to take small shares of this lucrative bargain, and so become parties to their own ruin?

Did not you and the solicitor of the bill endeavour to deceive and impose upon Parliament, by delivering into the Committee false statements and false lists of names of proprietors and occupiers of land, &c. through which the intended Canal was to be cut? And when the unfair means you were practising were detected, and the scheme rendered abortive, did you not suffer those deluded persons to pay their quotas of the expenses, except only a few *choice friends*, whose assistance you thought might be serviceable to you in your future views and designs on the borough?

Have you not deserted your colleagues, the very respectable and consistent Members of the county of Berks., and joined Mr. Fox, and the Coalition Faction, through private pique to Mr. Pitt, or for some other (and what) reasons?

Did you not uniformly support the Faction in their unconstitutional attempts to invest the P[rince] of W[ales] with the Regal Authority, independent of Parliament, without restrictions or limitations, or providing for His Majesty's reassumption of his government, on his recovery from his indisposition?

Was not you the mover, and Mr. Fox the seconder, of a motion to re-examine the K[ing]'s Physicians, in expectation of finding His M[ajesty] was much worse than the daily accounts given by them to the public seemed to indicate, in hopes to obtain such terms for the P[rince] as would enable his intended

Ministers to lavish the public treasure and *splendid titles* on themselves, and such *time-serving adherents* as could be tempted to betray their kind and good master in the hour of his affliction?

Did not you, after having perused a copy of the Abingdon Address to Mr. Pitt promise the Mayor of that town to present the same?

Why then was it beneath YOUR *dignity* to present it in the usual respectful manner, when several noblemen and gentlemen of ancient and respectable families have not thought it any disgrace to do so, in compliance with the wishes of public bodies of men, to convey their grateful acknowledgements to the Minister for the many essential services he has rendered his country?

Have you not expended, since you have represented the borough of Abingdon, many thousand pounds at Cirencester, Oxford, and other places, equally distant from Buscot, in articles which could have been supplied on as good terms by your constituents?

What were those *weighty*, and *powerful* arguments you made use of to prevail with certain gentlemen of Abingdon, so soon to alter their opinion of your *merits* and *deserts*, and forget the many promises and public declarations they had made, 'that they would never more interfere in contested elections for that borough;' and with another gentleman, who had assured a friend of mine, that in the meditated opposition of Captain Bowyer against you, 'he would observe a STRICT NEUTRALITY? But, strange to tell! these *very consistent gentlemen*, in a few days after, appeared with you on a public canvass, and if I am rightly informed, have since privately exerted *every art* to gain proselytes to your unpopular cause. Let the motives for such conduct be what they may, which induced these gentlemen to forfeit their boasted loyalty, patriotism, and veracity, the impartial public will fix an indelible stain on their characters, which time itself shall scarcely obliterate.

                                                              TRUTH.

London, April 20, 1789

N.B. Shortly will be published, 'A Succinct Narrative of a Transaction at Faringdon, when a Lease, executed by a *certain Gentleman* to Farmer ——, was infamously cancelled, without his Consent'. Also, 'A Treatise on a New Mode of paying Turnpike Tolls, as practised by a *Commissioner*. With some curious Anecdotes from Wales, never yet printed'. Berks RO, Preston MSS A/AEP/11.

---

36 Dissatisfaction with the conduct of the MPs for Derby, 1823

Pop c 17,000 and a freeman electorate of c 650. The Duke of Devonshire and the Coke family had the strongest interests in the town. At the 1826 general election, Henry Cavendish— the Duke's first cousin—was re-elected, but Mr Coke was not.

W. J. Lockett to [James Abercromby—a Devonshire Agent]
20 March, 1823

One of the most urgent subjects upon which I wish to confer with you, is the complaint now very generally and loudly made of the inattention of our Borough members to their parliamentary duty. Their names have not appeared in any of the divisions during the present session, and they could not be found or heard of last week when the petition from the town, relative to the Insolvent Debtors Act was to be presented to the House of Commons.

I informed you some time ago that observation had been made by several of the leading members of the Corporation and principal inhabitants on this subject. Mr. Cavendish's military duty, and Mr. W. Coke's feelings in consequence of his uncle's marriage, were urged in excuse for their want of regular attendance during the last session; but apologies on those grounds will no longer be admitted. It is now very plainly said by the best friends of both families, that if the members either cannot or will not attend to their duty, they ought to make way for others who will.

With respect to Mr. W. Coke, I am of opinion that even if he is inclined to offer himself again, he will not be returned for the borough. It is known that although he was in town frequently during the last session, when several important questions were brought forward, and was constantly in public, he would not enter the House of Commons. Both he and his father have been apprised of the consequences of further neglect, and yet he has been hitherto, during the session, at Melton.

Mr. H. Cavendish is not so much to blame, but the town is very far from being satisfied with the degree of attention which he has paid to his duty. The public eye is upon him also and you may be assured that if he is not at his post very regularly in future, it will be impossible to prevent him from sharing the fate of his colleagues Chatsworth MSS, 6th Duke's Group, 785.

37 A protest against Lord Lonsdale's use of his influence in Carlisle, 1816

Pop c 14,000 and a freeman electorate of c 700. Lord Lonsdale and the Duke of Norfolk both had very strong interests in the corporation. At the by-election in February 1816, John Christian Curwen, the Norfolk candidate, stood successfully against Sir Philip Musgrave. Dobinson here charges Lord Lonsdale with throwing his weight behind Musgrave. Wybergh was one of Curwen's agents.

William Dobinson to Lord Lonsdale

Carlisle, 18 March 1816

I have the honour to address your Lordship on a subject not only of considerable importance to myself and my fellow freemen of Carlisle, but of infinite consequence to your Lordship, and which a sense of duty alone prompts me not to overlook or disregard. Although a relative and friend of Mr. Curwen's, I make this communication to your Lordship unknown to him or to anyone, actuated by a sincere and earnest solicitude to secure at all times the free and constitutional representation of my native city against any undue influence, I am not to be deterred by menaces or overawed by power. Your Lordship I am sure will applaud rather than condemn the motives which induce me to trouble you. Your Lordship's secret and latterly avowed interference in the late contested election for this city was unparallelled in the annals of electioneering, and the solemn pledge of strict neutrality and indifference which was made to Mr. Wybergh ought to have been preserved inviolate. An open departure from such an obligation requires a clear and unequivocal explanation from your Lordship, otherwise it must in a great measure, shake the confidence of every man in any pledge, however solemnly given, that may be made by your Lordship—It is almost impertinent for me to remind your Lordship, that the better to secure the freedom of elections, no Lord of Parliament, or Lord Lieutenant has any right to interfere in the election of Commoners; this, my Lord, is a wise and salutary regulation of the House of Commons and demands your Lordship's serious consideration. Your Lordship's influence united with that of the Church and State was found light in the balance when opposed by the glorious spirit of Freedom and Independence which has been so conspicuous during the late election, and once more confirms, what has long been manifest to every enlightened mind, that the freemen of Carlisle, are not only quite competent to exercise their elective franchise without your Lordship's aid or assistance, but that they are resolutely determined on all occasions manfully to step forward to crush every coalition or alliance however formidably arrayed, which seeks to overthrow their dearest rights and privileges. The freemen of Carlisle have perfect confidence and dependence that Mr. Curwen will neither disappoint their expectations nor those of the country. Under the pledge thus solemnly given to Mr. Wybergh and by him communicated to Mr. Curwen's Committee your Lordship must be sensible that some explanation is called for to justify the line of conduct which your Lordship thought fit to pursue and that I have not wantonly or unnecessarily obtruded myself on your Lordship. It has been my anxious desire, as it is my duty, to express myself in decorous and respectful terms to your Lordship and I flatter myself your Lordship will condescend to favour me with a reply. I have considered it more advisable to address myself to your Lordship personally than through the medium of any public journal which may possibly never fall into your Lordship's hands. Lonsdale MSS.

38 Private elections for Marlborough and Great Bedwin in June 1793

Marlborough had a population of nearly 2,000 and a corporation electorate of about five. Near by, the smaller town of Great Bedwin had a burgage and freeholder electorate of about 120. Both were in the pocket of Lord Ailesbury, a local landlord. There were by-elections in both boroughs in June 1793: Lord Dalkeith was returned for Marlborough and Lord Courtown for Great Bedwin.

J. Ward to Lord Ailesbury
                    Marlboro', 30 June 1793, Sunday morning
My Lord,
    My Last gave your Lordship an account of our proceedings as far as to the close of the Marlborough Election poll which ended as satisfactory as possible. Their Lordships then proceeded to make the usual morning visits & I believe omitted no one who had need to be called upon: after which we dined together under a very commodious Booth as comfortably as could be wished and spent the afternoon in about as Loyal & Convivial a manner as was the case on the Rejoicings for the King's Recovery. In short every body appeared pleased & happy, & I suppose there never was an election at Marlborough which gave more general satisfaction, and at which the conduct of the Members & their companions were more entirely approved of. The libations & cheers which accompanied their Healths & those of your Lordship & Lady A., Lord & Lady Bruce, The King & Constitution &c &c &c produced such effects as I hope your Lordship will allow me to draw the veil over; they may be easily guessed—we were more merry than wise—but I never

witnessed more good humour on such an occasion—Dr. Majendie attended & seemed to enjoy a scene he had never before been present at. He spoke to me in the Handsomest Terms of your Lordship's conduct in 1790 respecting the Windsor Tithes & of your Late Concession, which was considered by the Chapter as so very liberal that they have enrolled your Lordship's Letter upon that occasion amongst their Records.

The Ball, as might be expected, was crowded & hot but the Dancers enjoyed themselves & everything went off very satisfactorily.

Yesterday morning we set off for Bedwin about 11 o'clock. Mr. Baverstock went in the Coach with Lord Courtown &c, who were in raptures all the way with the beauties of the Ride —They were received at the Marquis's Clump (which should be replenished next Winter) by the Garland Music Colours &c & Horsemen & conducted to the Cross Keys from whence we proceeded to election immediately. Mr. Baverstock's speech did not fall short of the expectations which former experience of his abilities in that way had raised, & his nomination was followed by an immediate & joyful concurrence of all present. We got to dinner by 2 o'clock in the Town Hall & were joined by my Brother, Taylor, Mr. Tom Hancock & Mr. Halcomb from Marlborough, & spent a very pleasant afternoon together. The affability & attention of their Lordships pleased everybody & when Lord Stopford* drank success to the Borough of G. B. & the worthy Electors with three times three, Farmer Bushell of Crofton threw the whole company into a convulsion of laughter & applause by exclaiming 'we'll choose you every year Sur; come when you wull'.

Their Lordships set off for Windsor about 5 o'clock with very steady drivers—The Dinners both at Marlboro' & Bedwin were very well dressed & the Wine was good—The three Lords desired me particularly to return their grateful acknowledgments to your Lordship for all your goodness & attention to

*Lord Courtown's son

them & left Bedwin with most favorable impression of Wil-
shire Hospitality, & Lord Dalkeith promised to visit the
Bedwinites again if Lord Stopford had occasion to pay them
another visit. Wilts RO, Savernake MSS, 9.

39 The bustle of an election in Durham, 1802

Pop c 10,000 and a freeman electorate of c 1,200. The
Lambton and Tempest families had the strongest interests in
this relatively 'open' borough. At this election, Richard
Wharton stood as an independent candidate with the hope
of breaking the Lambton-Tempest monopoly, and succeeded to the point of heading the poll with R. J. Lambton.
Later, however, his return was successfully contested by a
petition to Parliament alleging illegal practices.

Thomas Brand to Lord Bruce   Durham, 18 June 1802
... We came here before the dissolution that we might avoid all
bustle and tumult, and last night we were terrified out of our
senses. Mr Lambton had arrived in the evening to canvass to-
day and a mob of his friends and foes had assembled on the
occasion and were not yet dispersed when Mrs Brand, her sister
and I, who had been dining about 7 miles from Durham, came
home in the dark. Unfortunately Mr Wharton's mob recog-
nising a Wharton carriage and mistaking me for their hero
were proceeding to take off the horses and drag us to the house
in triumph, but the dexterity of our driver saved us. When they
found their mistake they were more quiet but they accompanied
with loud huzzas in honour of the family and when I got the
ladies safely lodged I was forced to hallow Wharton for ever
and toss up my hat with theirs. The poor ladies, most nervous
at best, were some time before they recovered. Mr Wharton is
in great spirits and I think he shall have a majority of 150 but
Mr Lambton is now on his actual canvass and I fear this very
day will decant these filthy dregs from our bottle to his. I am
sorry to say we have not half a dozen *gentlemen* with us. Wilts
RO, Savernake MSS, 9.

40 Bribery at Leominster, Herefordshire, 1796

Pop c 3,000 and a 'scot and lot' electorate of c 550. Leominster was a relatively 'open' borough with a tradition of 'riot and drunkenness', according to *The Times*. At this election John Hunter, an East India Company director, was opposed by the Duke of Norfolk's candidate, Robert Biddulph, and Lord Malden's, George Pollen. The following extracts are from an electoral roll annotated by Hunter's agent, George Coleman, and recording payments made to the voters. Hunter and Pollen were returned.

Voters	Occupation	B[iddulph]	H[unter]	P[ollen]	Paid £	s	d	Unpaid £	s	d	Agent's Comments
R.											
Ross Thomas,	Yeoman	1									
Ravenhill William,	Baker	1	1					5	5		
S.											
Seward Robert,	Baker		1	1				5	5		
Stephens John,	Joiner	1		1	"	"	"	"	"	"	
Saul Joseph,	Turner	1	1					5	5		
Seaborne John,	Joiner	1	1		3	3		2	2		
Spencer Thomas,	Shoemaker	1	1		5	5					
Seaborne William,	Carpenter	1	1		4	4		1	1		due to Mr Coleman
Stonely John,	Miller		1	1	5	5					
Sandland Thomas,	Yeoman		1	1	5	5					
Smith Thomas,	Mason	1	1		5	5					
Scandret James,	Taylor	1	1		5	5					
Southall Samuel,	Mercer		1	1	x	x	x	x	x	x	Quaker
Simpson Thomas,	Gent.		1	1	x	x	x	x	x	x	Gent
Smith Thomas	Shoemaker, South St.	1	1		5	5					
Sanderson Christopher,	Gardener		1	1	5	5					
Starie Thomas,	Cutler		1	1	x	x	x	x	x	x	A Man of Property
Stockton John, Sen.	Yeoman, (Blind)		1	1	4	4		1	1		
Still William,	Labourer	1	1		5	2			3		due to S. N.
Smith William,	Watchmaker		1	1	5	5					
Shepherd John,	Labourer	1			"	"	"	"	"	"	

Voters	Occupation	B [iddulph]	H [unter]	P [ollen]	Paid £	s	d	Unpaid £	s	d	Agents Comments
Sandland Edward,	Basket-maker	1	1					5	5		
Southall John,	Mercer		1	1	x	x	x	x	x	x	Quaker
Strainge John,	Butcher			1	,,	,,	,,	,,	,,	,,	
Soloman, Henry,	Cutler		1	1	5	5					
Scarlet Charles,	Hatter	1	1					5	5		
Scarlet Edward,	Grazier	1	1					5	5		
Sayer John,	Staymaker	1	1					5	5		
Scarlet J. jun.	Farmer	1			,,	,,	,,	,,	,,	,,	
Scarlet John,	Gent.	1			,,	,,	,,	,,	,,	,,	
Sheward Joseph,	Mercer		1	1	x	x	x	x	x	x	A Man of Property
Seaborne Robert,	Joiner	1		1	,,	,,	,,	,,	,,	,,	
Spencer John,	Saddler	1	1		4	15	6		9	6	

Summary of total payments

		£	s	d
150	Paid in full	787	10	0
109	in part	363	6	0
	Rem. Due	208	18	7
135	not yet paid any	708	15	0
68	Gent.	0	0	0
462		2,068	10	0

	£	s	d
Deduct sum p^d in p^t as above	1,150	16	5
Yet due to Voters	£917	13	7

	£	s	d
Due to Mr Coleman	458	19	1
Do to Voters	917	13	7
Total	£1,376	12	8

41 How the voters voted in Newark, Nottinghamshire, 1790

Pop c 6,500 and a 'scot and lot' electorate of c 650. This

document gives a clear indication of the relative strength of the various families and of the ways in which their tenants voted. The Duke of Newcastle was the lord of the manor of Newark.

	[The Candidates]					
	Crosbie & Sutton	Crosbie & Paxton	Sutton & Paxton	Paxton	Sutton	Total
Newark						
[*Landlords*]			[*Tenants Votes*]			
His Grace the Duke of Newcastle	197	33	3	28	—	261
The Right Honble. Lord Middleton	10	1	1	2	—	14
Sir Jennison Gordon	9	—	3	14	—	26
Mr. Rastall	9	4	4	33	—	50
Messrs. Tomlinsons	4	—	1	30	—	35
Mr. Fillingham	5	—	—	1	—	6
Mr. Jessop	7	2	2	9	—	20
Mr. Calcraft	3	1	1	4	—	9
Mr. Guthrie	7	—	—	5	—	12
Mr. Handley	6	—	1	1	—	8
Voters .... in right of their own houses	22	2	4	8	1	37
	279	43	20	135	1	478

Number of voters at the election in 1790: 645

| Rejected [votes] | 71 | 12 | 8 | 162 | | 253 |

Nottingham Univ Library, Newcastle MSS NeC4500.

---

42 Some results of a poll-book analysis. Malton, Yorkshire, 1807

Pop c 3,000 and a 'scot and lot' electorate of c 600; see (34) for the general background.

(i) The voters can be divided into three groups:
  (a) Professional people and wealthy businessmen and tradesmen, being 20 per cent of the total;
  (b) Tradesmen, being 65 per cent of the total;
  (c) Labourers, being 15 per cent of the total.
Landlord influence and money played the largest part in determining the result of the election but it is interesting that class (a) voted as follows: for Cooke, 52 voters; Dundas, 46; Headley, 33; Leatham, 16.

Class (c) voted as follows: for Headley, 42; Leatham, 29; Dundas, 26; Cooke, 13.

(ii) Only 57 per cent of the Fitzwilliam tenantry voted for Dundas and Cooke; although, if the votes cast for either Cooke or Dundas in conjunction with one of the other candidates are added, the percentage rises to 76 per cent. It was because of the thin support given to the Fitzwilliam candidates that recalcitrant tenants were later punished.

43 Dealing with erring tenants in Newark, 1831

See (41) for the general background. William Tallents, the Duke's agent, is here referring to the 1830 election when the Newcastle candidates, Michael Sadler and Thomas Wilde, were beaten at the poll by Henry Willoughby. Some seventy-seven of the Duke's tenants voted for Willoughby and Wilde; one of these is referred to in the following letter as deserving punishment. The Duke's political evictions caused a good deal of indignation in reforming circles, coming as they did just as the first Reform Bill was being debated.

W. E. Tallents to the Duke of Newcastle

Newark, 22nd April, 1831

Many of the tenants who were under notice to quit at the present Lady Day are overholding and set me at defiance, so that those to whom I had let the houses, having given up what they were occupying, are put to great inconvenience until the refractory tenants quit. Wherever the parties under notice had at the last election of Mr. Sadler given him one vote and the other to Mr. Serj. Wilde, I have endeavoured as far as I could do it consistently with my promise to the new intended tenant, to allow them to continue, but this has rarely occurred because the new tenant has in general made arrangements which disabled him from releasing me from my promise.

The house occupied by Thorpe the confectioner in the Market Place, about which you have had repeated applications from

him (once through Sir Robert Bromley) to permit him to continue, I had let to a person named Sutton who wishes to have
it, but would give up his claim if *that* be the only obstacle to
Thorpe being continued tenant.

Now Thorpe has a wife and large family—the house was re-
built for him about two years ago and he and his father lived
in it for more than half a century. Yet this ungrateful fellow
voted for Wilde and Willoughby, for which he pleads having
been made drunk, and urges the largeness of his family, the ruin
consequent upon his leaving his situation and his contrition for
the past, and promises of amendment for the future.

I have given him no reason to suppose he will be permitted
to remain, but have deemed it right to submit all the circumstances to your Grace, and to await your directions. Nottingham Univ. Library, Newcastle MSS, NeC 4526.

---

44 Election expenses at Harwich, 1807

Pop c 2,700 and a corporation electorate of thirty-two. The
government through its admiralty influence had the strongest
interest, although it was only slightly stronger than that of
Lord Sidmouth. At this election Addington was Sidmouth's
nominee (they were brothers) and Huskisson that of the
government.

---

*Expense at the Election of the Rt. Hon. J. H. Addington and William
Huskisson Esq. to represent the borough in Parliament*

	£	s	d
To ringers	5	5	0
To Chairman	8	8	0
To constables	7	7	0
To Serjeants at Mace Hall. Keeper & Cryer.	4	4	0
To Water Bailiffs	1	1	0
To music.	4	1	0
To dinners for ringers, Chairman and constables.	13	13	0
To flagsmen and boys.	5	18	0
To Do. on board the packets, custom & excise and other vessels, shipyard, Naval officers, & several other houses etc. }	3	6	0

	£	s	d
To Mr. Jermyn & men assisting the Chamberlain.	1	1	0
To chairs	4	4	0
To Mr. town clerk's fees.	10	10	0
To Mr. town clerk for stamps	4	0	0
To bills for ribbons	47	18	0
To Mr. Bull's bill.	125	2	6
To express to Mr. Addington to Kelvedon	1	7	0
To Serjeants to attending Mr. Addington and Mr. Huskisson.	1	1	0

£248 6 6

BM Add. MS 38759 f 179.

45 A general account of the Maldon election in 1826

Written on behalf of one of the candidates, Thomas Barrett
Lennard. Pop c 2,300 and a freeman electorate of c 1,400.
The result was: Hon. G. Winn 1,747; Thomas Barrett
Lennard 1,451; Quinton Dick 1,401.

Minutes of Maldon Election 1826

On Wednesday 7 June 1826 commenced one of the severest
struggles for the representation of the Borough of Maldon that
was ever known, Mr. Thomas Barrett Lennard, Honble. Mr.
Winn and Mr. Quintin Dick were the three candidates. The
severity of this struggle was occasioned by the *coalition* formed
between the parties of *Winn* and *Dick* to defeat Lennard the
Whig candidate; and what created greater difficulty, after all
the Burgesses who were enrolled upon the books previous to the
election were polled, the Mayor, C. C. Parker exerted himself
to the utmost by attending *early* and *late* to give every facility to
the admission of every one having the *shadow* of a claim to the
freedom; the consequence of such facility being given to the
admission of Freemen the extraordinary number of 1800 were
added to those already upon the books, which swelled the
amount of voters to about 3200. On Wednesday the first day of
the Election Mr. Lennard was proposed by Mr. Osgood Han-
bury seconded by Mr. John May—Mr. Winn by Colonel

Bramston, seconded by Sir John Tyrrell and Mr. Dick by Mr. J. S. Nance, seconded by Mr. Thomas Bygrave of London. The principles avowed by the Candidates left little doubt that Mr. Winn and Mr. Dick were Tories; while Mr. Lennard declared sentiments of the most liberal character, of which the country had before them the experience of his last 6 years Parliamentary conduct, which he should not deviate from nor was he one of those men that would refuse to give His Majesty's ministers support when he considered their conduct deserved it, and he did not hesitate to say he saw much in His Majesty's Government to approve, particularly as related to the foreign diplomacy of the country; for it was highly gratifying to see that confederacy of Kings evidently brought together to destroy the liberty of the people beaten down by the determined conduct of Mr. Canning. Such conduct he unhesitatingly declared deserved approbation and he should feel pleasure in giving such conduct, let it come from what party it may, his decided support. The other Candidates declared themselves generally the supporters of those principles which have brought the country into its present perilous state, that any relief to the Catholics must be attended with danger to the Established Church, and without Church and State united in one common bond, this country could not prosper—in fact the whole of their speeches amounted to this—*no retrenchment*— no *reduction* of *sinecures*—*no reduction of taxes*, as without the present enormous amount the public credit could not be supported and the dignity of the country maintained. On the subject also of Colonial slavery Mr. Winn explicitly declared it having been sanctioned by Government for many years the proprietors of West India property have as good a property in their slaves as any gentleman had in his estate and he did not see why their title should be disturbed, more than the proprietor of the soil. That with respect to Parliamentary reform, the present House of Commons was a good representation of the people and he should oppose any innovation upon it. With those who dissented from the Established Church he thought no innovation or repeal of the present penal statutes ought to be sanctioned, as the present establishment of Church and King had long been the admiration of the world. Mr. Dick went but little into an explanation of his sentiments except that he was friendly to the present Government and that if he was returned to Parliament he was determined to give every opposition in his power to any further concessions being made to Roman Catholics which would be dangerous to the Church of this country upon which mainly depended the happiness of it. Upon a show of hands the Mayor declared it to have fallen upon Mr. Lennard and Mr. Winn—Mr. Dick having demanded a poll, the freemen commenced enrolling their names that at the close Mr. Lennard was very considerably at the head. This occasioned a coalition between the parties of Mr. Winn and Dick which was first formed on the Thursday and continued until Friday evening when it was broken off. On Saturday another offer was made to Mr. Lawrence the accredited agent of *Mr. Winn* by Mr. Fisk of Witham an attorney employed by Mr. Dick, when Lawrence told him Mr. Winn having pledged himself *personally* not to coalesce with either candidate, it was impossible he could give his assent, but that his Committee and friends would readily do so. So that in fact with the exception of Mr. Winn's personal interference, every engine was put in force to oppose Mr. Lennard: and the expenses of Mr. Winn were to be paid by Mr. Dick from Monday 12 June. That Mr. Winn though he did not personally interfere actually allowed his committee to sell his interest to the other party at the price of being cleared from all future expenses. What can be a greater proof of connivance and privity on the part of Winn thus allowing himself to be thrown into Dick's pocket. On Thursday the second day every exertion was made by the Blue Party from Dengey and Rochford Hundreds every workhouse ransacked for voters every influence exerted, every person capable of being brought to Maldon to make a show was forced forward to assist that coalition our majority of the preceding night had induced them to enter into. To give every aid to the polling in favour of the 2 Tory candidates, Mr. Parker the Mayor with the insignia of his office suspended from his *neck*, actually left the hustings and under the pretence of keeping peace in the Polling Booth, assisted the voters to the poll, showing them the Clerk before whom they were to register their votes. The motive of such corrupt and partial conduct could not but strike the by-standers with disgust and induced Mr. Payne one of the bur-gesses to accuse the Mayor of placing himself in the polling booth for the purpose of influencing the voters as they came to be polled. Aware he was a considerable holder of land in the Hundred from which a great number of them came and also Chairman of the Board of Magistrates for that division of the county, he remained there a very considerable time handing up the voters in the interest of Winn and Dick. On the next morning Friday, he saw Mr. Payne upon the hustings when the latter stated he was so very ill with an inflammation upon his chest that it was not possible for him to remain upon the hust-ings, and retired to the Committee room for the purpose of remaining there during the day. A short time after Mr. William May came to the Committee room and informed Mr. Payne the Mayor intended to appeal to the freemen upon the insult he had yesterday received from him, who had accused him of partiality and corrupt motives in appearing among the freemen in the poll booth the day before, and also of corrupt practices on the part of constable. Mr. Payne immediately pro-ceeded to the hustings to hear the charge of Mr. Mayor, who after endeavouring to defend his character, upon the ground he had *not asked a single voter for his vote* and that he went into the booth, supposing the men did not know where they were to vote, began by defending the constables particularly *Brown* the *borough Reeve* of whom he said a more impartial person could not be found in the discharge of his duties. Mr. Payne replied to him by stating that though in private life he had a great re-gard for the Mayor, he would not be deterred as a freeman from speaking his sentiments of any man whom he saw a public officer in the discharge of his duty guilty of conduct that deserved reprobation and he could not refrain from saying he never saw any of a more flagrant nature than that which he observed in the Mayor on Thursday who was under the pretence of handing voters to the poll too ignorant in his opinion to read *the letters of the alphabet under which* they were perfectly aware they were to poll. But why should he descend from the dignity belonging to the office of Mayor and mix himself up with the voters except it was to promote the ends of the party, while every voter was attended by partisans ready to lend their aid in getting them to the poll. The motive was intelligible enough to every one versed in electioneering contests. He was the Chairman of the Magistrates of the Dengay division. He was also a considerable holder of land from the very district these voters came from and coupled with other facts of the Mayor's conduct left no doubt in his (Mr. Payne's) mind of the motives that actuated his conduct the preceding day which he Mr. Payne would not hesitate to designate as below the dignity of any returning officer and disgrace to the Magistrate of the Borough. With respect to the Borough Reeve and other constables he would say the most shameful and barefaced partiality had been practised by them in throwing any impediment in the way of Mr. Lennard's friends coming to the hustings while *persons* wearing the colours of the other candidates though *not free* were allowed every access to the Poll. The Mayor here interrupted Mr. Payne and the affair dropped, but to show the truth of Mr. Payne's observations, Mr. Mayor no more appeared in the Poll Booth and he detected such improper conduct on the part of his Borough *Reeve* that induced him to suspend him from his office. The admissions of Freemen went on from 8 o'clock in the morning to 8 in the evening, at other times not exceeding four o'clock. The hour of closing the poll, this also depended upon the capriciousness of the Mayor who if he knew of a supply of voters coming into the town for Mr. Dick was sure to prolong the time for closing the poll, to give them an opportunity of getting admitted; that Mr. Dick might appear better at the close. Not so for Mr. Lennard, for in several instances when we expected coaches from London, the poll was closed *at 4 o'clock*, and the fair presumption to be drawn is that the Mayor had some information of their being expected. Indeed, no trick he could play off was spared, when he thought it would be done effectually for Dick's interest. The Coalition formed by Mr. Winn's agents and committee for the purpose of electing Mr. Dick, there can be little doubt of, was with the connivance of Mr. Winn, for what committee would attempt, without the approbation of the principal, to undertake entering into an arrangement for splitting votes and sharing expenses. After the professions of neutrality and friendship several times made publicly to Mr. Lennard by Mr. Winn, the terms *insidious* and *unnatural* used by Mr. Honeywood cannot be considered harsh. If any further proof of Mr. Winn's being accessory to the coalition was needed, it can only be necessary to mention the fact of his meeting Mr. Dick at Mr. Lawrence's (Winn's accredited agent) on Sunday 11 June, the day before the avowed coalition; from thence he went to dine with Mr. Newmans, the clergyman of Witham, where a voter came for certificates, and Mr. Newman in *Mr. Winn's Presence* requested him to vote for *Winn* and *Dick*, Mr. Winn making no objection to such a division of vote; if he had expressed an opposite wish to Mr. Newman, the man would have voted for Mr. Winn solely. It can never be for one moment believed that Mr. Charles Parker, Colonel Kesterman, Captain Spitty and many others who are known to be decided partisans of Mr. Winn would have coalesced with Mr. Dick unless they knew privately it was not disagreeable to Mr. Winn, as surely men moving in the first of gentlemen would be careful how they subjugated the principal of their *party* to observations from the country at large which cannot be otherwise than injurious to him as a gentleman for members in the County can never be satisfied that Mr. Winn did not connive at the coalition and as Mr. Western justly and forcibly expressed himself as a party man he should have respected the declaration of his principal and as a principal he would have abjured the party that would not so have respected

his avowal of neutrality. The conduct of the clergy generally
has been such as to leave a very unfavourable impression upon
the minds of every independent man; what can be worse than
their partial conduct with respect to the granting certificates
necessary to prove the titles of many applicants for their freedoms. In many instances the orange interest was compelled to
send agents under the Tory colours or they had no chance of
getting the necessary documents . . . I shall always look upon
this struggle as one made upon the part of the Tory interest
to try their strength through the purse of Mr. Dick. They
cannot but feel disappointed at the result having showed they
are incompetent to carry into execution what has always been
the boast that they could return two members for the *County*
and *borough*. It now appears if the votes are all reduced to
plumpers, [single votes] it will be found Mr. Lennard polled
1238, Mr. Winn 1068, Mr. Dick 800, so that a great majority
of persons evidently appeared in favour of Mr. Lennard. How
then the Tories can fancy it is in their power to return two
members I am at a loss to guess, for I firmly believe had a
second Whig candidate offered himself, a great many of Mr.
Dick's voters would have polled for him, while nearly all our
plumpers would undoubtedly have split with the two Whigs.
Another circumstance operated very much against Mr. Lennard, viz. his inactivity for a long time previous to the election,
having scarcely ever canvassed, while Mr. Winn saw personally
almost every voter. The result of this battle has destroyed the
borough as a *county one*, and the chances are members from
London will for the future be selected as the only individuals
who can *afford* to contest the place. It is evident from the state
of the poll the neighbourhood of Maldon is where Mr. Dick
derived his strength; the popular cry had more effect near the
borough than anywhere else; that popularity will not *continue*;
the same inducement to vote for him *will never again happen* for
the wish of voting under the impression their votes would not
be good unless they were enrolled, influenced very many to
poll for Dick, that will never do the *like again*. The folly of the

Tories was never surpassed. What could be greater than to encourage a stranger to prolong the contest which must under any circumstances be ruinous to their county candidate, and prevent his ever offering himself again from the fear of having to sustain another ruinous contest, with a certainty of never having a quiet seat, with two Tories returned for so populous a borough as this; in which perhaps a more independent party scarcely any borough can boast, fairly marshalled in the mysteries of electioneering, and holding a regular communication with the Whig gentlemen of the county, who consider it of the first political consequence to return a Whig candidate for Maldon. The Corporation being as exclusively in the hands of the Tories, is to a certain extent injurious, particularly as it gives them an opportunity of selecting the returning officer, who if he proves partial, as was the case with Mr. Parker, gives a great advantage to the party. His conduct must lower him in the estimation even of his friends; it must convince them he rarely acts upon any fixed principles . . . Had he conducted himself as he professed, friendly to the county men, much of the struggle might have been obviated, but scarcely had the conflict commenced when without any reason, he turns a determined enemy to Mr. Lennard, and in the most barefaced manner enters the town as the returning officer accompanied by his servant weaving the double colors (sic) of *Winn* and *Dick*. With his horse he drove decorated with *Party ribbons*; such an indecent spectacle perhaps never before presented itself . . . The indirect countenance given to the partial behavior (sic) of the Constables, opperated (sic) very injuriously to us; our voters were on the 2nd and 3rd day much retarded, when coming to the poll while every facility was given to those who appeared with the Blue colors. And in too many instances, it was visible the manner in which the constables canvassed the voters when they came . . . to poll and by the order of the Mayor, preventing the friends of Mr. Lennard speaking to those in his interest whom they were conducting to the poll. In spite of all these obstacles, and fighting with the greatest odds against us, the Whigs were successful, which nothing but the determined spirit of the party could have given the most sanguine partisan reason to suppose would have been the result. But undoubtedly there is a strength amongst the middle class of persons in this county in support of liberal principles which if well managed and fostered by the Gentlemen of the county would turn the character of it from that which now disgraces it—of being always subservient to a few leading tories possessing no abilities to warrant their leading any party . . . Essex RO D/DL 042/3.

Section three: LARGE AND POPULOUS CONSTITUENCIES

46 Stewarding at Westminster, 1788

Pop c 150,000 and a 'scot and lot' electorate of c 12,000. Westminster was the largest and foremost urban constituency in Britain, and from the 1770s was the scene of repeated contests between well-organised radical interests and those of the government of the day. At this by-election, the government and Sir William Young supported Lord Hood against the Foxite whig, Lord John Townshend. Townshend won by over 800 votes.

Sir William Young to the Marquis of Buckingham

10 August, 1788

At dinner, in Downing Street, I was requested to take 'my day or two station' on the hustings; it being necessary to have some gentlemen there who might notice procedure, and prevent the high bailiff yielding in every case to the most abject fears on every threat of Mr. Fox, which he did, insomuch that Lord Apsley and myself were obliged to threaten him with a prosecution. On the hustings were posted a set of young men, neatly dressed in blue and buff for the occasion, blacklegs from all the race courses, and all the Pharo and E.O. tables in town. Their business was to affront every gentleman who came on the hustings without their livery. 'You lie!' 'Who are you? damn you!' and a variety of such terms echoed in every quarter; something of the sort soon tingled in my ears. On observing a dirty-looking man encouraged to swear, and not mind *that fellow*, meaning your humble servant, I could not refrain expressing my disgust, at hearing even invitations to a disregard of perjury; on which, Counsellor Garrow, of Newgate education, addressed me with, 'damn your eyes and limbs! and who are you, who give yourself these airs?' Having made up my mind to put a stop, *in limine*, to such mode of address, I gave him my card, and told him we had better settle the rest of the business elsewhere, 'and immediately'. He was for the first time in his life abashed, and made excuses, which I gladly enough accepted; . . . I have mentioned the above anecdote, as characteristic of the deportment of the blue and buff for special purpose of clearing the hustings; and too often they succeeded, occasioning moderate men, who did not choose to commit themselves to withdraw; and thus getting whole divisions of the hustings to themselves, where they polled every beggar from the streets. The question is not of title to vote in most cases, but of identity; most families being at this season out of town, a rascal was found to personate every absentee. The suborners of perjury not regularly conferring, very many instances occur of an absentee being represented by four or five, *all* admitted to vote on their mere attestation. Duke of Buckingham ed. *Court and Cabinets of George III*, 1, 417–18.

---

47 Electioneering at Liverpool, 1812

Pop c 104,000 and a freeman electorate of c 2,700, of which number a substantial majority were working people. Merchants on the corporation also possessed considerable weight, although they rarely acted in a body in a constituency which was notorious for its venality. In 1812, for example, Henry Brougham was supported by some merchants as the spokesman for the corporation's case against the orders in council which had severely damaged the city's trade; others, however, supported George Canning, Brougham's opponent, and a member of the government that had introduced the orders. Canning stood with Isaac Gascoyne and Brougham with Thomas Creevey. Brougham and Creevey retired together.

Brougham to Earl Grey

Croxteth Park, Friday, 16 October, 1812

I have just come here from the Liverpool election, which is over at last. I could have kept it up a week longer, polled 150 more votes, and made the enemy spend £10,000 more (he has, I suppose, spent £20,000 already), but finding myself infinitely popular with *both* parties, from my manner of conducting it, and preserving the peace of the town in an unprecedented manner (which they ascribe wholly to me), and having not a shadow of chance of beating them, they being already 200 ahead, and having as many unpolled as I had, I gave in with a good grace at 12 to-day; and have had the SATISFACTION of being assured by the enemy how happy they would have been to return me, if we had rested satisfied with one [seat]. I do not regret our taking the other choice; we ran them amazingly hard. On Sunday last they would have compromised; on Monday they thought themselves quite beaten, and on Tuesday; but on Wednesday things looked up, though Gascoyne only passed me yesterday at one o'clock. The fact is, they all renewed their subscriptions, and said if £50,000 were required they were resolved to do it. They gave twenty and thirty guneas a vote, and the thing was done. Our friends have not spent £8000, and sums are still flowing in from all parts; £400 only a hour ago came from Glasgow, and as much from Hull, and the Birmingham folks swear that they will *buy* me a seat, but of course this is a way of speaking. Indeed if I cared much for popularity, I may well be gratified, for never was anybody so supported, and the enemy has *only the votes*; they who polled against us crying out to us that their hearts were with us, but they dared not. The starting two [candidates], inflamed and combined our adversaries, and made the two parties (Corporation and Tories), with a large secession from the Whigs, unite against us. The miracle is our having made such a fight; and they look gloomy on their own victory, because they know to what they owe it.

You can have no idea of the nature of a Liverpool election; it is quite peculiar to the place. You have *every* night to go to the different clubs, benefit societies etc., which meet and speechify. This is from half-past six to one in the morning at least; and you have to speak to each man who polls, at the bar, from *ten* to *five*: It lasted eight days. I began my canvass three whole days before, and had nine nights of the clubs, besides a regular speech each day at close of the poll. I delivered in that time *160* speeches and odd; and yesterday and to-day, after being beaten, I rallied, and delivered regular speeches to the whole multitude. I had to close with one above an hour long, so you may guess how exhausted I am, especially as I never saw a popular election before, and knew nothing of it.

The exploits of the Whigs were my chief subjects, and I flatter myself I have done much to reclaim the people there. Yesterday I preached on Pitt's conduct and immortality, which was prodigiously well received; and to-day I concluded with a long profession of adherence to Fox and his friends, with reasons, etc., which was far better taken than I had expected by the people; indeed, perfectly well received, and most extremely well by the upper classes. These two, being, of course, the only things I took any pains with, will be put in the paper, and you'll see them. As to any proceedings of a more violent nature, our party had so much the possession of the town, after the first day, that there was no facing us; some scuffles occured afterwards, but except a throwing of stones (in which young Roscoe and I had narrow escapes), we never were in any danger: some few accidents happened, two or three men being killed, and others severely cut and wounded, but all who knew Liverpool formerly say nothing was ever seen so quiet at an election there. The enemy had a disposition to row me *personally*, and set a broken *slave captain* on me, who acted at Canning's bar, but he found it would not do, and retreated. A man of a more respectable description was also set on me, and in consequence of my treating him *loudly* on the hustings, sent me a letter which reached me just as I was beginning my speech; but having a friend who had joined me there for the purpose, I sent him to say I did not seek a quarrel, but I had not the least wish to avoid one, etc., which produced an ample written apology. These things are, of course, between ourselves, especially the last, as the man is in the customs, and I should not wish to injure him, believing him to have been set on. There was much squibbing, but all on our side except a very extraordinary one—attacking me as given *to unnatural practices*. The utmost industry has failed in discovery with author, printer or circulator, but it came from some of the underlings of *Canning's* friends. I never saw a man so *astounded* as Canning was when I told him of it, & I believe he would have given half his votes & more to have got rid of it—indeed they all were equally annoyed by it. You may guess *how much* this annoyed *some* of them, but I expressly forbade all retaliation on a pledge being given to help in finding out the authors and circulators.

So now you have as accurate an idea of the humours of the election as if you had seen them, and at a small cost. The zeal of our friends is inconceivable, and in some cases melancholy; one has been in confinement, having actually gone mad; several others have *ruined* themselves; and they have already formed a committee, etc., for bringing me in next vacancy, but we expect no opposition. Brougham MSS, partially printed in *Memoirs of Lord Brougham*, vol 2 (1872), 61–5.

———

48 Organising an election at Westminster, 1818

See (46) for the general background. In May 1807 the radical interest in the constituency was managed by the Westminster committee, a large body composed mainly of tradesmen who sponsored a candidate of their choice and organised his electioneering for him. This committee was re-activated at each successive election and by 1818 was firmly under the influence of the radical tailor, Francis Place. In the preparation for a by-election in 1819, the committee joined with the City whigs in supporting John Cam Hobhouse and the following documents illustrate the especially detailed work of organisation that it undertook with Place's supervision. In the event, the whigs and the committee split, and Hobhouse was defeated by the whig candidate, the Hon. George Lamb.

(a) *Election of John Hobhouse Esq. Recommendations to the Parish committees etc.*

As many electors as can be procured are to form themselves into a Parish or ward committee.

If more than one committee be formed in a Parish, they are to correspond in the most intimate manner possible, and mutually to assist and support one another.

A Public General meeting must be called as soon as possible.

Resolutions should be passed at those meetings.

A person should be engaged by the committee as Secretary, he should be paid not exceeding 7s. per day, [and] he must be punctual in his attendance.

A room must be engaged by the committee.

The committee should appoint several of its members to act as Chairman every one of whom when he takes the Chair should remain in it until relieved by some other member.

The committee to report to the managing committee every day at an hour to be agreed upon and more often if need be.

The committee will be furnished with the following books, viz.

1. A Minute Book, in which everything done should be entered.
2. A copy of the Rate Book as furnished during the last Election—This Book must be corrected by the actual inspection and enquiries of the canvassers, and the numbers of all the Houses should be inserted therein.
3. A canvassing Register—into this Book must be copied the name and address of every canvasser, and the description of the Book he uses.
4. A complete set of Canvassing Books. These when used if not returned in a reasonable time must be sent for.

5. A Printed copy of the Poll Book interleaved with writing paper.

All information under the heads inserted as directions to the canvassers should be inserted in the Parish Rate Book for which a space has been left.

(b) *Canvassing*

The most important of all things is a correct and vigorous canvass. Every means must therefore be used to induce Gentlemen to become canvassers. Every canvasser must be requested to go from House to House and report to the committee on as many particulars as possible.

1st. The number of all the Houses.

2nd. Those kept by women.

3rd. Those kept by foreigners.

4th. Whether a promise or a refusal.

5th. Every receiving House for general or two-penny Post letters.

All these and every other particular worth noticing should be written on the canvassing Book with pencil and not ink or with ink on a separate paper. Canvassers should use the canvassing cards carefully, and return those not used. It is recommended that at least two canvassers go together.

(c) *An advert in morning papers*

Westminster Election.

The Managing Committee for conducting the election of John Hobhouse, Esq., sit daily at the Crown and Anchor Tavern in the Strand, to whom all communications are requested to be addressed.

The Parochial Committees meet daily at the following places:

St. Anne . . . King's Arms, Old Compton St.

St. Paul & St. Martin's le grand . . . Shakespeare Tavern, Great Russel [sic] St.

St. Clement & St. Mary . . . Red Lion, Haughton Street, Clare Market.

St. Martin . . . Griffin, Villiers Street & Coach & Horses, St. Martin's Lane.

St. James . . . Great Room, 40 Brewer St.

St. George . . . King's Arms, Duke St., Grosvenor Square.

St. Margaret & St. John . . . Red Lion, Princes St., Westminster.

Subscriptions are received at all the foregoing places and by
the Treasurer, Mr. S. Brooks, 110 Strand, Edward Langley,
Esq., 176 Edgeware Road, and Mr. King, 22 Charing Cross.

Signed: S[amuel] Brooks

(Chairman)

(d) *General Report of the State of the different canvassing Parties,*
29 Dec. 1818

J. Smart, Inspector.

St. Anns . . . Understood to be fully canvassed but no returns
made.

St. Clement . . . One Party out this day—some progress made
in the canvass but no returns, expected to make a return in
part to-morrow.

St. Pauls . . . Nearly all canvassed with great precision but
nothing doing at present. Returns duly made to this time.

St. Martin . . . Just beginning to be active, no returns yet, about
10 Books out to-day with canvassers.

St. James . . . Canvassing not quite finished, returns made in
part.

St. George . . . But little canvassed, at present wholly inactive.

D? outward . . . But little done, expect to make up one or two
parties to-morrow.

St. Margaret . . . Much to do, nothing doing, returns regular.

BM Add. MSS 27847 ff 25–6, 37, 41.

---

49 A fierce contest at Leicester, 1826

Pop c 26,000 and a freeman and 'scot and lot' electorate of
4–5,000. There was a long tradition in Leicester of trials of
strength between the corporation, representing strong tory
views of a 'Church and King' variety, and the radical and
nonconformist interests, which flourished particularly amongst
workers in the woollen industry in the borough. At this

E

election—when two tory squires, Sir Charles Hastings and Robert Otway Cave, represented the corporation, and William Evans, a millowner, and Thomas Denman, the London barrister, the interests of the reformers—the Catholic question was a vital issue. Catholic emancipation implied nonconformist emancipation with a consequent revolution in the structure of the corporation. The framework-knitters also constituted an important element in the electorate, and (b) suggests one of the reasons why Cave and Hastings received about 40 per cent of their votes at an election which they were eventually to win.

_____

(a) *Handbills from the candidates*
(i) A Few Questions [from Hastings and Cave]

Who deprived the King of England of his Crown, and gave it to the Pope? *The Papists.*

Who burnt the Protestant Bishops and Martyrs, in Smithfield, &c. in 1555? *The Papists.*

Who hatched the Gunpowder Plot to blow up the King and Parliament of England in 1605? *The Papists.*

Who butchered two millions of Protestants in France, on St. Bartholomew's Day, in 1572? *The Papists.*

Who set up, and now maintain, the bloody Inquisition in Spain? *The Papists.*

Who perpetrated the cruel Irish massacre, when two hundred thousand Protestants were murdered, in 1641? *The Papists.*

Who raised the rebellion in Scotland, in 1745? *The Papists.*

Whom did King George the Third kick out of his Cabinet (with disgust) for trying to overthrow our Protestant Establishment? *The Papists.*

Whom did his Royal Highness the Duke of York swear to exclude from his Councils? *The Papists.*

Who withold the freedom of election from the boroughs of Horsham and Steyning? *The Papists.*

Who have hired a French newspaper to traduce and vilify the English nation? *The Papists.*

Who then will vote for the Roman Catholics?
None but those who are enemies to our good old English
Church and State.

(Leicester, June 19, 1826)

(ii) Worthy and Independent Electors of the Borough of
Leicester.

Gentlemen,

I am compelled by the gross and absurd calumnies which are
every where circulated respecting me, to address to you a few
words on the subject of the Catholics Claims. I have no intention of entering into the details of a question which has already
been fully discussed. I think it necessary solemnly to declare
that, so far from having any inclination to favor the doctrines
or the influence of the Roman Catholic Church, I feel the
strongest aversion to both; and that I think all its distinguishing
tenets theologically unsound, and politically dangerous. It is
because I am convinced that our present system, by degrading
the intellects and exasperating the passions of our Catholic
fellow-subjects, tends only to increase and perpetuate the
bigotry and disaffection which it is designed to suppress; it is
because I am convinced that conciliatory measures alone can
diminish its malignity and hasten its final extinction, that I
approve of those lenient and liberal propositions which have so
frequently received the concurrence of the most eminent States-
men, and have repeatedly been sanctioned by the House of
Commons.

Under these circumstances, I cannot see any reason to
apprehend that the admission of twenty or thirty Catholics to
seats in our legislative or executive Councils would, in any
degree, endanger a Church which is securely founded on the
word of God, on the principles of sound reason, and on the firm
and devoted affection of a great people. My opinion may, no
doubt, change. New reasons may be brought forward. New
circumstances may occur. It is possible, though, I think, most
improbable, that the Catholics, after their admission to political

power, may prove themselves unworthy of it by conduct dangerous to our religion and constitution. Should such be the case, no fear of being reproached with inconsistency and vacillation shall deter me from performing the duties which will then devolve on a Protestant legislator, and from concurring in the simple and easy measure of revoking concessions so ungratefully abused. But till that time, constrained by a sense of public duty, to which every selfish feeling and interest ought to bend, I must continue to support those wise and conciliatory propositions which I at present think essential to our repose at home, to our authority abroad, to the prosperity of the people, the stability of the Church, and the dignity of the throne.

I remain, Gentlemen,

Your obliged and very faithful Servant,

Leicester, June 3rd, 1826.   *William Evans*

(Cockshaw, Printer, High Street, Leicester)

Leicester Museum and Reference Library, Leicester Election Papers (1826).

(b) *A statement from the Framework-knitters Society*

To the Framework-knitters

Fellow workmen,

It is with peculiar gratification that we have to announce to you the handsome donation of FIFTY POUNDS from Mr. Otway Cave, to the Framework-knitters' Society. This reasonable donation, when from depression of trade, and the lowness of your wages, you can scarecely pay the interest of that debt which you have contracted, we hail, as the earnest of those exertions Mr. Otway Cave will make in the Senate House, to restore you to a State of comfort, if he is so fortunate to be returned as one of the Representatives of the Borough of Leicester in Parliament. As it respects the *repeal* of the CORN LAWS, he stands on the *foremost ground*—that repeal he has pledged himself to support and which he justly considers is 'the STEPPING STONE to the removal of other abuses'. We think him deserving our *entire* confidence—we ask for him that confidence from you, convinced that he will strictly fulfil the pledge he has given, and that he is *the sincere friend of civil and religious liberty*. We cannot entertain a doubt upon this subject, and the impression which your patience and resignation under those sufferings of which he has been an eye-witness during his canvass, and which he has seen with deep regret, will long be engraven upon his heart. In soliciting your votes for Mr. Otway Cave, we consider that we are fulfilling that duty which we owe to you and to our country.

Signed: E. Nicholson } Jewry Wall District
J. Dilkes

W. Johnson   Sanvey Gate District
J. Simpson   3rd Belgrave Gate District
R. Wiggins   2nd Wharf St., District
E. Barradell   Elbow Lane District
T. Rawson   North Gate Street District
J. Ellicock   Church Gate District
H. Ward   1st Wharf St. District
J. Godfrey   1st Belgrave Gate District
J. Pendleton   Bakehouse Lane District
E. Dann   } Oxford Street District
T. Brandreth
T. Turnes   London Road District
T. Clarke   2nd Belgrave Gate District
J. Hart
W. Kenrey   } Knotted Branch
E. Gartett
John Jones   Loom Branch
                Thomas Clark
     Chairman of the Framework Knitters Committee
Leicester, May 31st.
   Leicester Journal (2 June 1826).

(c) *The election proceeds*
At the close of our last publication, there was not the least ray of hope, that the Corporate Body would be able to bring any

Gentleman forward in their interest, at the ensuing Election. The Town Clerk, after having been several days in London, without attaining the object of his mission, returned on Friday morning. During the week a letter had been received from Sir Charles Abney Hastings, of Willesley Park, on some business respecting the Election which the Town Clerk deemed expedient to be discovered in person. He accordingly proceeded to Willesley Park during Friday, and ultimately succeeded in obtaining Sir Charles Hastings' consent to become a candidate. On Saturday morning, the Mayor and Magistrates, with other members of the Body (in seven carriages) waited upon Sir Charles at his residence, and after having partaken of the hospitalities of the mansion, returned, accompanied by the worthy Baronet in his carriage and four, escorted by a considerable number of Electors on horse-back. On entering the town, the horses were taken from Sir Charles's carriage, and he was drawn in by the populace. When arrived at the bottom of the High Street, the cavalcade was met by Mr. Evans's friends on their return from canvass; a tumult in consequence ensued, and several windows of the Stag and Pheasant Inn, (the rendezvous of Sir Charles's committee) were broken; a child was killed during the affray—and some persons seriously injured; but peace was restored during the night. On Monday morning a handbill was published by the Mayor and magistrates, expressive of their determination to preserve the peace of the town; and to prosecute the persons already in custody, and others who might be guilty of similar offences. The same morning Sir Charles Hastings, accompanied by the magistrates, and a very numerous assemblage of respectable electors, proceeded on his canvass of the Exchange, attended by a military band, and a very splendid Blue and White Banner, elegantly decorated, with motto's illustrative of the principles he professes—as a zealous advocate for 'The Church,—King, and Constitution'. Sir Charles has met with the most flattering assurances during his canvass and no doubt is entertained by his friends, of his ultimate success. On Wednesday, Mr. Otway Cave finished his canvass; Mr. Evans continued to canvass yesterday. Both Gentlemen were surrounded by friends warm in their interests, and each evening there were very large assemblages of the populace to hear their different addresses; but to the credit of the town at large, there has not been the least disturbance since Saturday night, although the different parties have frequently come in contact. *Leicester Journal*, (26 May 1826).

PART THREE

County and Burgh Elections in Scotland

INTRODUCTION

As in Wales, each Scottish constituency returned one member to Parliament. Of the Scottish counties, six returned members by a system of rotation for alternate Parliaments only: the 33 counties therefore produced 30 MPs for each Parliament. This left the return of 15 burgh members. Edinburgh returned one, but the other 14 were elected by 14 groups or districts: 5 of these were made up of 4 burghs and 9 of 5. Thus, in 1830, Scotland's population of 2·9 million was represented at Westminster by 45 MPs.

This rather complicated system of representation was based upon equally complex county and burgh franchises, making the Scottish electoral system quite unlike those of England, Wales or Ireland. In each county the franchise (and indeed the qualification for an MP) belonged first to those who possessed 'in property or superiority' freeholds of 40s of 'old extent'—that is, of freeholds so valued at the end of the thirteenth century. This qualification was said to embrace, during this period, land valued at more than £70 in rent, and therefore excluded the small yeomen and farmers. Secondly, it included those who owned land held of the Crown 'in property or superiority' worth £400 Scots (or c £35 sterling) in valued rent.

The key word in both cases was 'superiority', which described the state of vassalage to the Crown. The right of voting was attached to that state, and as the property which went with it could be conveyed to others, it enabled those who possessed a great deal of property in superiority to make it and the vote over to others, and thus create for themselves personal electoral interests. This particular franchise was subject to a number of variations and, as document (51) illustrates, a vote could be made up of land valued as property (without superiority) and as superiority (without property). However, despite the complications of the system, the results of both qualifications were clear enough. They excluded the two social groups which were electorally influential in England—the middling gentry and small farmers—and gave the vote to only 2–3,000 individuals. This in turn meant that county elections were contested in each case by rarely more than a handful of people, as is illustrated in documents (50, 53, 54). Furthermore, as the voting qualifications depended upon complicated estimates of property valuations, success or failure could turn upon such mundane matters as the careful scrutiny of electoral lists, illustrated in document (52). Political debate derived from conflict between the interests of different social and economic groups was, therefore, not a feature of Scottish county elections. They could, of course, turn on the political views of individuals but such was the nature of politics at the social level from which they were drawn that the scramble for patronage and place was a much more enduring fascination. It was this factor, which gave the government of the day such considerable power in the Scottish representative system.

The franchise and the method of election in the burghs was even more unusual, being based upon a two-tier system. At an election, each burgh council elected a delegate, and the delegates of all the burghs met and elected the MP. In those districts which contained only four burghs, one delegate possessed two votes. Thus, those who controlled the councils controlled the delegates and therefore the election. Furthermore, as the councils were small with usually fewer than twenty members, their history depended upon the same factors as prevailed in the smaller English close boroughs. In fact, about half submitted to pretty continuous management during this period, while the others were largely influenced by the flow of cash. William Adam's survey of some burgh prospects at the 1806 general election (55) illustrates the kind of calculations inspired by this situation.

Section one

50 A general view of Scottish electioneering in a 'Fair statement of Northern Politics' of March 1786
The Gordon and Fife interests dominated Banff's electorate of 120 and accounted for about eighty of the 180 voters in Aberdeenshire. In Murray (Elginshire), however, their earlier supremacy in an electorate of about eighty was being challenged by the Murray Association. Eventually a general agreement was reached covering the three shires, which resulted in the defeat of the Fife interest in Elginshire in favour of the Grants.

1st View. It is perfectly clear that the Duke of Gordon united with Lord Fife can carry without any Battle or Bustle.

    1mo/   The County of Banff

    2do /   The County of Murray

    3dly.   They are superior to any other Interest yet formed in the County of Aberdeen.

    4thly.   By the Duke's getting Lord Kinloss's Boroughs of Kinloss & Inverurie those joined to Banff which is believed now under Fife's Direction would carry that District.

    In the View therefore of a Coalition between the Duke and Lord Fife, it Remains for the Treasurer to consider what would be an Equitable Partition.

2nd View. Supposing the Duke to unite with Mr. Brodie and the Murray Association and to be opposed by Lord Fife, Findlater & ye Grants

    1mo/   They carry by the Reduction of Fife's entailed Votes but after a strong Battle ———— Banffshire.

    2^{ndo}/   They also expect to Carry Murrayshire

    3dly.   They Annihilate his Ldps Power in ———— Aberdeenshire. By this last Arrangement, the Duke gets the

Benefit of Their success in Banff and Aberdeenshire; In Consideration of His Joining ye Party, in Murrayshire. By the 1st Arrangement with Lord Fife, Peace and Success go together, in Banff and Murray Shire; without Recourse to any other Ally.

By the 2nd Arrangement, with the Murray Association, a hard Battle is to be fought in Every County, and Success Purchased with Hasard & Expence; Besides Obligations to Various Individuals.

But what chiefly Recomends the *last* Arrangement is that it Renders the Duke's Political Power more Permanent, by lessening Fife's Numbers in *all* the Counties, in Perpetuity— And Therefore, some Risque ought to be Run, and Expence Incurred—nay, even a Temporary Advantage given, for obtaining that Object.

3rd View. If Sir James Grant or Lord Findlater could be withdrawn from Lord Fife, the *Second* Arrangement In Opposition to Fife, appears clearly, most Eligible for the Duke to adopt.

BECAUSE

It would insure success in Banffshire, Annihilate Lord Fife's Power in Aberdeenshire, and aid the Attack on Murrayshire: Besides, attaching Sir Jas. Grant to the Duke, in Inverness Shire.

To Accomplish therefore, this Detachment of Lord Findlater & Sir James Grant, or either of them, from Lord Fife, falls to be managed by The Treasurer's Address—But as It seems material, in deciding the Preference Between the different arrangements, the following Hints are humbly offered.

The Duke to apply for Lord Kinloss's Boroughs of Kinloss & Inverurie to Mr. Alex. Brodie, and *He* to make an *oriental* attack upon ye Town of Banff, or to get Elgin.

And Sir James Grant to have Murray Shire with the support of the Duke, Findlater and the Association.

The Duke to Procure for Sir James, Lord Kinloss's Boroughs, which with Cullen, or Elgin, makes him sure: and then, A. Brodie to have Moray. But it is believed Lord Kinloss would prefer the *first* Mode of ye Disposal of *his* Boroughs Because it would be giving to them, a Member *Independent* of Ld. Findlater.

At any rate, it is submitted, if the Duke should not so far Profit of his Friendship with Lord Kinloss, as to get him, to stipulate in any future Transfer of his Boroughs, that Lord Findlater should give no opposition to the Gordon Family, in Banffshire; By Reducing The Duke's Votes, or otherwise. NLS MS 5, ff 16–17.

Section two: COUNTY ELECTIONS
51 Qualifying for the vote in Kinross, 1805
One of six shires that elected a member in alternate elections. It had a population of c 7,000 and an electorate of between seven in 1788 and twenty-three. This document shows the complicated details of voting qualifications.

Matthew Sandilands to William Adam

Edinr., 14 Sep. 1805

I have examined the titles upon which your father & you stood upon the Roll of Freeholders of the County of Kinross and I find your father stood enrolled upon the following lands partly superiority and property, and partly superiority only viz:

		£	s	d	Valuation. £	s	d
The four quarters of Blair—Property—					242	9	1
Dullomuir	— Do. —				21	5	$0\frac{2}{3}$
					£263	14	$1\frac{2}{3}$

And parts of Nivingstone possest by

		£	s	d			
John Curror	Superiority	66	0	$0\frac{2}{3}$			
Henry Flockhart for D. Horn	Do.	34	5	$10\frac{2}{3}$			
John Herdman (Quarryhead)	Do.	5	18	8			
Wm. Livingston	Do.	10	18	8			
James Livingstone	Do.	20	2	2			
					137	5	$5\frac{1}{3}$
					£400	19	7

And your vote is on:

		£	s	d	£	s	d
Dowhill	Property	£247	19	1			
Diekindad	Do.	100	0	0			
		347	19	1			
Dowhill Mill	of Dowhill superiority	55	13	9			
					£403	13	1 [sic]

And you have valuation upon your
Blair Estate

	£	s	d	Valuation. £	s	d
Kinnaird, purchased from Mr. Rolland	191	8	3⅗			

And the following superiorities:

	£	s	d		£	s	d
Robt. Curror, ⅓ of Easter Nivingston	£33	0	0				
Do. Cleesh Mill	7	18	4				
Mr. Dalling	5	2	11½				
John Livingston (Murrayknow)	10	17	10				
John Meldrum	9	7	10		66	6	11⅓
					£257	15	3
Riley					66	13	0

And your son Charles has:

	£	s	d		£	s	d
Balingall	£88	0	0				
Gairney Bridge	68	11	2				
					156	11	2
Total Valuation belonging to you } and your son Charles }					£1,285	12	1

If you wish both your sons John & Charles to be upon the
Roll of Kinrossshire, it is believed that altho' the Blair estate
be now entailed that you could give your son Charles the
superiorities at Nivingston by selling them to the vassals, and
by then conveying them to Charles and there would remain
valuation sufficient of the property lands as would complete a
vote to your eldest son without touching your own vote, and
which you might dispose to him notwithstanding the entail.
    Viz:

	£	s	d
The four quarters of Blair	242	9	1
Kinnaird, purchased from Mr. Rolland	191	8	3
	£433	17	4

And Capt. Charles's vote to consist of

	Valuation.		
	£	s	d
Balingall & Gairney Bridge his own property	£156	11	2
Riley	66	13	0

And the following parcels, if you
have right to the superiority only,
and not to the property also.

		£	s	d
1.	John Curror $\frac{2}{3}$ of Nivingston Easter	£66	0	0$\frac{2}{3}$
2.	Henry Flockhart for D. Horn	34	5	10$\frac{2}{3}$
3.	John Herdman (Quarryhead)	5	18	8
4.	Wm. Livingston	10	18	8
5.	James Livingston	20	2	2
6.	Robt. Curror $\frac{1}{3}$ of Easter Nivington	33	0	0
	do. Cleesh Mill	7	18	4
7.	Mr. Dalling	5	2	11$\frac{1}{4}$
8.	John Livingston (Murrayknow)	10	17	10
9.	John Meldrum	9	7	10
		£426	16	6$\frac{2}{3}$

This would be sufficient valuation for your son Charles, but
I am not altogether certain if your father did not purchase the
property of some of these superiorities. I suspect he purchased
No. 2, marked Henry Flockhart, but of this Mr. Bruce will be
able to inform you, or it could be discovered by examining the
valuation of the Cess of the Parish of Cleesh as it *now* stands in
the Cess Books. If No. 2 is now your property and that you
cannot give it to him, the remainder would be short of a qualification to him by about £8 . . .

I had some doubt whether your titles to the Estate being now
the late Entailed Titles did not annul your former Title on
which you stand on the Roll of Freeholders of the County of
Kinross and thereby lose to you your place on the Roll. I took
occasion to mention this to Mr. Rolland, and he is of opinion
that it did not . . . Blair Adam MSS, General Correspondence
1805 S-Z.

52 The registration of votes in Kincardineshire, 1808
Pop c 25,000 and an electorate of between fifty-five and
seventy-five. Lord Melville, Mr Barclay of Urie, and
William Adam all had strong interests in the shire. Adam
was elected in 1807. Because electorates were very small and
the franchise complicated, the checking of qualifications was
a crucial aspect of electioneering.

Matthew Sandilands to William Adam
                                            Edinr. 24 Sept. 1808
On receipt of yours from Thorney Abbey I wrote to Mr. Low
to send me here copies of six of the claims for Inrollment in
Kincardineshire which I suppose to be the claims of enemies,
and I wish they may come in time to enable me to make the
necessary searches of the records here. They are:

G. Harley Drummond, Esq.   of Stanmore (Middx)
Alexr. Munro, Esq.   (without designation)
Alexr. Duthie, Esq.   of Ruthrieston
William Farquhar, Esq.   of Balhamhill, County of
                           Surrey
Wm. James, Esq.   of Caleaton Street, London
                           Merch.
Gavin Hadden, Esq., Mercht. of Aberdeen.
If you consider any in the above list to be friends, let me
know ... Blair Adam MSS, General Correspondence 1808 H-Z.

-----

53 The electoral register for Haddingtonshire, 1788
In 1788 the whigs found themselves in possession of a report
giving every useful political detail about the 2,662 voters in
the Scottish shires. It was compiled for the use of William
Adam, one of the whigs' electoral managers and, as the
following extract for Haddingtonshire shows, could be of
inestimable value. The report stated that the leading interests
amongst the seventy-five voters in the shire were:

1. The Marquis of Tweeddale, brother-in-law to the Earl of Lauderdale. Opposition.
2. The Earl of Hopetoun. Ministerial.
3. The Earl of Wemyss, formerly Mr. Charteris, whose son, Lord Elcho, is attached to Opposition.
4. The Earl of Hadinton. A moderate man. Inclined to support Government. His only son, Lord Binning, is married to a sister of Lord Hopetoun.
5. Mr. Nisbet of Dirleton, who has a very large estate. Married an English lady, a Miss Manners, daughter of Lord Robert Manners. Has an only daughter.
6. John Hamilton of Pencaitland, brother of the last. Present Member for the County. A good estate. Married a niece of Mr. Dundas.*
7. Mr. Hay of Drumelzier. A good estate. Married a daughter of Mr. Erskine of Cardross. Will probably go with the Marquis of Tweeddale.
8. Sir David Kinloch of Gilmerton, Baronet. A great estate. His family Opposition principles, and it is thought will go with Opposition, though his sister is the mother of Hamilton of Pencaitland, the present Member.
9. Sir Hew Dalrymple of North Berwick. His son, Hew, once represented the County. Has an office during pleasure of £300 or £400 a year in the Excise. A great estate, and great expectations from Mr. Hamilton of Bargany in Ayrshire. Was brought into Parliament chiefly by the Buchans, his relations, and may go with them.
10. Mr. Buchan Hepburn. A Lawyer. Married the widow of General Fraser. Had children by a former marriage. He and his father have a great estate, and pretty good interest, in this County. He wants a Judge's gown.

and of the individual voters

* Henry Dundas, 1st Viscount Melville, (1748–1811) who managed Scottish elections for Pitt's government.

24. SIR DAVID DALRYMPLE, Baronet.
   Lord Hailes in the Court of Session. Independant man.
   Married a sister of Sir Adam Fergusson's. Will go with the
   Dalrymples in this County.

25. PATRICK LINDSAY of Eaglescarnie, in right of his wife.
   Independant in circumstances. A daughter married to the
   late Lord Blantyre. Will go with that family, who, it is
   thought, will lean to the Marquis of Tweeddale.

26. JOHN CHRISTIE of Baberton.
   Now divested. The vote belongs to David Anderson of St.
   Germains, the great friend of Mr. Hastings. He made his
   money in India, and is in very affluent circumstances; and
   married a sister of Finlay of Drummore. His brothers, John
   and Francis, are Writers to the Signet; another brother a
   merchant in Edinburgh.

27. SIR JOHN SINCLAIR of Murkle, Baronet.
   Now succeeded by his son, Sir Robert, who married his
   cousin, Lady Magdalen, daughter of the Duke of Gordon.
   He has a good but not a very large estate, and is the
   Ministerial Candidate for the County of Caithness against
   Sir John Sinclair of Ulbster. He is a relation of Dundas's.

28. JAMES HAMILTON of Bangour.
   Married a sister of Bruce, the Abyssinian. Always abroad.
   Pretty independant. A near neighbour, and friend, of
   Buchan Hepburn.

29. SIR JOHN ROSS, Baronet, of Balnagowan.
   Married a neice of Dundas's. Son in the Army; one in the
   Navy. Son lately married a daughter of Count Lockhart.

30. CHARLES DALRYMPLE of Winterfield.
   A brother of Sir Hew aforesaid. Married a widow whose
   family he is interested to provide for; one of them, George
   Dalrymple, a Captain in the 42nd, known well to Prince
   William Henry; the other, a Major in the Army, Aide-de-
   camp to the late Duke of Rutland. This family it is thought
   will go with the other Dalrymples.

31. JOHN M'DOWALL of Logan.
Married a sister of Buchan Hepburn's father. His son Member for Wigton. A good estate of £2000 or £3000 a year. Ministerial.

32. ROBERT SINCLAIR, Esq., Advocate.
The uncle of Sir Robert Sinclair aforesaid. Made a Clerk of Session by Dundas. Will go with him.

33. HEW DALRYMPLE, Younger of North Berwick.
Disqualified by an office in the Excise. Before mentioned; see Sir Hew.

34. SIR ANDREW LAUDER DICK of Fountainhall.
Married a daughter of Broun of Johnstonburn. Has a good estate of £2000 a year. Will be directed by George Cumin, W.S., his cousin.

35. JAMES WILKIE of Gilkerston.
A small estate. A great family. He is Manager of the Royal Bank at Hadinton. He will lean to the Buchans and Mr. Ramsay of Edinburgh.

Sir Charles Elphinstone Adam ed. *The Political State of Scotland* (Edinburgh 1887), 160–1, 164–5.

___

54 The election for Dunbartonshire, 1821

Pop c 27,000 and an electorate of between forty-three and sixty-five. The death of Archibald Campbell-Colquhoun in 1820 caused a by-election. A near relation, Sir James Colquhoun, 3rd Bt, decided to stand on his interest in December when the state of interests was as follows:

___

	votes
Duke of Montrose	20
Duke of Argyll	7
Sir James Colquhoun	5
Doubtful (but likely to vote for Montrose)	2
Doubtful	4
Not to vote	5
	43

SRO, Melville Castle Papers GD51/1/198/8/7.

———

The Lord Advocate, William Rae, took a hand in putting up John Buchanan of Ardoch as Colquhoun's opponent with the support of the Montrose interest, and on 9 January informed Lord Melville:

———

According to a note which Lord Succoth has handed me, the matter stands thus:

Declared for (J. Buchanan of) Ardoch	21 [votes]
Donald will be got	1
	——
	22
	——
Exclusive of new votes to come on Sir James [Colquhoun] may, and probably will have	15
Three new Elphinstone votes viz.	
Sir P. Malcolm, Wm. Adam, Mr. Lock, if good	3
Peter Speirs vote if sustained by Court of Session	1
Young Gartmore if he can claim as heir apparant	1
	——
	20
It is understood that the Lord Chief Commissioner is denuded but if not	1
	——
	21
	——

N.B. There may be an objection to one of Ardoch's votes, also to the three new Elphinstone votes. But this should be kept quiet. Mr. Edmonstone will carry the Presses.
SRO, Melville Castle Papers GD51/1/198/26/54.

———

At the election Buchanan won by six votes out of thirty-four cast.

Section three: BURGH ELECTIONS

55 The government's hopes in six Scottish burghs at the 1806 general election; this took place in November

William Adam to Lord Grenville [Prime Minister]
(copy)   Edinburgh, Friday 24 Oct. 1806

I have found on my arrival here much to do in the general affairs & much in my own—& very considerable possibility in both. I will first state the general affairs and the measures which I am induced to hold in consequence of yr. Lordps. note and frequent conversations with me.

1.   *Edinburgh* [pop c 80,000 and an electorate of 33. Sir Patrick Murray was elected on Lord Melville's and the Duke of Buccleuch's interests as an opponent of the government.] 'Mr. Mansfield is in the north of Scotland and does not move forward as a candidate. The other party here have not yet found one—and many members of the Corporation, finding that this City requires the co-operation of Govt. are reported to me as being inclined at once to support a friend of yr. Ldp. They tell me that for these last three days my name has been universally mentioned—but this is only in my opinion symptomatic. What I intend to do is visit the members of the Town Council, who are the electors, individually—and to ask them whether they wish to support Govt., that they cannot be held to do so if they support Ld Melville's candidate, whoever he may be. That if they agree to my proposal, a fit person shall be found and the city will receive the aid of Govt. in its objects. My accomplishing this and writing after(war)ds would have been impossible. I will state the result tomorrow.'

2.ᵈ *Lanark Burghs* [Selkirk, Lanark, Peebles, Linlithgow which together possessed a population of c 12,000 and an electorate of 4 who were chosen by about 90 councilmen. The Duke of Hamilton had the commanding interest in Linlithgow and Peebles while the Duke of Buccleuch and Sir

Charles Ross controlled Lanark and Selkirk. The election
was decided by the vote of the presiding burgh which in
1806 was Lanark. Maxwell was therefore beaten. Mr.
Freemantle was the government's election secretary.] 'I
have written to Mr. Freemantle the measures essentially
necessary for that Burgh—and I hope they will meet yr.
Lorps. approbation. There is a great awkwardness in Mr.
Maxwell not being here. Ld. Lauderdale should send to
him to go off directly or if his health prevents, to send or
appoint a proper substitute to canvass for him. It will be
very vexatious if after yr. Lop. has given the interest (sic)
and thereby certainly disobliged Sir C. Ross, Mr. Maxwell's absence shd. frustrate the object.'

3^d. *Dundee Burghs* [St. Andrew's, Forfar, Perth, Dundee and
Cupar which together possessed a population of c 50,000
and an electorate of 5 chosen by 134 councilmen. Wedderburne had the commanding influence and at this election
returned himself.] 'On this too I have written to Mr.
Freemantle. I think with due exertion, by seeing the
Leaders in the Burghs and declaring the support they will
have if friendly—and the reverse, if hostile—(which I shall
do in terms sufficiently guarded), we shall be able to dis-
lodge Sir D. Wedderburne. This is near my field of action
and I shall be able to write more fully when I get to the
spot.'

4th *Dumfries Burghs* [Annan, Dumfries, Kirkcudbright, Lochmaben and Sanquhar; pop c 16,000 and an electorate of
5 chosen by 95 councilmen. The Duke of Queensberry had
the principal interest and was able to return the Advocate,
Henry Erskine.] 'The town of Dumfries has offered itself
to Ld. Armadale. The town of Kirkudbright is in the hands
of Ld. Selkirk. These two will be ready to chose delegates
to support the Ld. Advocate. The third town, Lochmaben,
can be got. Considering your Ldp's anxiety to have him in
Parlt. and the uncertainty still hanging over it, I have
authorized his relation, the Crown Agent, Mr. Inglis, to

come forward in his absence to represent him. If we get Delegates friendly to him chosen, we shall be easily able, if he is better secured, to provide another person to fill his place. The Advocate is still at Buxton. Our friends here dispond extremely about his health . . .'

5th *The B(ur)ghs of Dingwall &c.* [Dingwall, Dornoch, Kirkwall, Tain and Wick; pop c 12,000 with an electorate of 5 chosen by 82 councilmen. The government successfully persuaded Lord Seaforth and Lady Stafford to return Col. Mackenzie.] 'Lord Stafford has Dornoch. Ld. Seaforth, Dingwall. Mr. Laing, the Advocate and celebrated historian, has Kirkwall. Sir J. Sinclair, Wick. Sir C. Ross, Tain. It is not known here who Ld. Stafford and Ld. Seaforth support. But if it is open to them to support any one of yr. Lordps. friends, we can get Mr. Laing to unite in favour of such (a) friend. All that will be necessary is that delegates who will support such (a) friend, when named, be chosen. His name I wd. not mention at present further than this, that if (the) Lord Ad(vocate) is unsuccessful—he shall be that friend. If I am—I shall. If both unsuccessful, the Advocate for the motives which actuate yr. ldp. on that subject to have the preference. This can only be concerted in England by yr. Ldp. writing to Ld. & Ly. Stafford and by Ld. Carysfort bringing Ld. Seaforth to yr. Ldp.'

6th *The Inverness B(ur)ghs* [Forres, Fortrose, Inverness and Nairn; pop c 15,000 with an electorate of 4 chosen by 72 councilmen. Sir James Grant controlled two of the burghs including the presiding burgh in 1806. He therefore returned his son in Cumming's place.] 'Upon this subject, Lord Sidmouth shd. see the present member, Mr. Cumming and get him to stand again or name a friendly candidate. The Advocates (Henry Erskine) absence, and there having been no persons to direct here, puts many things in the greatest state of awkwardness—and I fear a good deal in risk. If I had been here a month ago with the authority yr. Ldp. gives me, and the confidence you place in me, much might have been done. But it is vain to look back. I mention it because I feel my responsibilities strongly— and am only comforted by knowing the candour & liberality of the mind I have to deal with in yr. Ldp.—and think I precisely understand the way in which you wish me to execute the powers, from our last conversation particularly.

Blair Adam MSS, General Correspondence 1806, E-K.

PART FOUR

Irish Elections

INTRODUCTION

THE two important features of the Irish electoral system during this period were, first, that in a largely Catholic country Catholics could not vote in elections until 1793 and could not be MPs until 1829; and, second, that the Act of Union between Ireland and Britain in 1801 abolished the Irish Parliament, reduced the number of Irish MPs from 300 to 100 and transferred them from Dublin to Westminster. The other relevant results of the Union were: (i) that the county representation remained unchanged with each of the thirty-two counties continuing to return two members; (ii) that by a process of selection, based upon assessments of wealth and population, the number of boroughs returning members was reduced from 117 to thirty-three; (iii) that the number of members elected by Trinity College was reduced from two to one; and (iv) that the franchise in both the counties and the boroughs remained unchanged.

In all this upheaval, the county representation was least affected. The qualification to become an MP and to obtain the vote were the same as in England until 1829, when Catholics were permitted to sit in Parliament and, as a quid pro quo, the minimum Irish franchise was raised from a freehold of 40s to one of £10. Thus, until 1829, Irish MPs were drawn almost entirely from the Anglo-Irish and Protestant ascendancy—a group that owned most of the property in Ireland and which in social terms was closely connected with the landed classes in Britain. On the other hand, the vast majority of voters were drawn from the tenantry. As far as their economic standing is concerned, research suggests that the average tenant holding in the more prosperous parts of Ireland was between 10 and 20 acres; in the less prosperous parts it was probably less. As for religion, it is clear that Catholics were enfranchised in large numbers after 1793 and that they composed the great majority of the 200,000 voters registered at the end of the Napoleonic wars.*

Thus for most of this period Irish county elections were concerned with relations between the Protestant ascendancy and an increasingly Catholic electorate. For a time (and certainly up to 1812), the landlord was able to exercise much the same influence as he had done before Catholic enfranchisement in 1793, and in some respects this seems to have been of a more powerful character than was the case in England. For example, there are good reasons for thinking that the Irish '40s freehold' was the more abused tenure as far as electoral matters are concerned. In England the freehold could be measured for value against the land tax assessments. Since a freeholder was unlikely to overvalue his property for tax reasons, there was a check upon freeholders with land worth less than 40s getting away with a vote. In Ireland there was no land tax. Furthermore, the less secure tenure of a lease for the duration of one, two or three named lives (which qualified for the vote in both countries) was more common in Ireland. Both these factors made it more possible for the Irish landlord to temporarily add a life to an otherwise yearly lease and so make a qualified voter out of a tenant. Moreover, it was equally possible that the tenancy was worth less than 40s per annum. Such a tenant became for electoral purposes a 'fictitious freeholder' and, if created upon a large scale, they could and did give a landlord an obedient body of troops which he could deploy during an election and then disperse.

However, while it is important to take note of the evidence

* The total county electorate rose from c 46,000 in 1784 to c 160,000 in 1803 and to c 203,000 in 1815. After 1829 it dropped to c 37,000.

relating to the existence of 'fictitious freeholders' (56), it is equally important to exercise some caution in estimating their influence. Successive acts of the Irish Parliament sought with some success to control their creation, chiefly by establishing a system of registration unique to the electoral history of the British Isles during this period. Furthermore, Irish landlords traditionally exercised a more powerful influence over their tenantry than was the case in England. This was because of their position as protectors of something more than their property; the increasing competition for small holdings; and the position of the tenant, which, if it cannot be represented as oppressed, may be said to have been, in many counties, depressed. It was most probably a combination of these factors, together with a more fluid land law, which made proprietorial interests stronger in Ireland than in England. In fact, it can be demonstrated that, until the advent of a strongly organised Catholic vote after 1812, most Irish county elections were determined by the most powerful proprietorial interests in a rather more authoritarian manner and with less reference to other considerations. Document (57) illustrates a proprietorial interest that was firmly based upon tenant strength, although the numerous body of supporters encouraged a compromise with the views of others. Document (58) illustrates the more absolute sway that Irish landlords could exercise.

It followed from the strength of the major landlords that 'independent interests' amongst the gentry and more substantial farmers were not a strong feature of Irish county elections. They were in evidence from time to time, as documents (59, 60) illustrate, but on the whole they provided a weak challenge to the authority of the great proprietors. The British government, on the other hand, as represented by the Irish administration in Dublin Castle, had a significantly coherent and definite role to play. Both before and after the Union, the Irish administration was charged with ensuring maximum support from the Irish MPs for English government. Furthermore, as the sole purveyor of patronage in both local and central government, it had an instrument of persuasion that was a potent force amongst the Protestant ascendancy. As a result, the chief secretary in the Irish administration was often closely involved in county elections. Sometimes, as is illustrated in document (61), he had a direct influence or, as in Co. Galway in 1820 (62), electoral interests came his way. Usually, however, he exercised the government's influence indirectly, as is illustrated in document (63).

However, the most direct and, in the end, the most successful opposition to the authority of the Protestant landlords came from the Catholic voters. In all but a handful of Irish counties, Catholics were in a majority and, as this numerical supremacy became slowly reflected within the electorate, they exercised an increasing influence in elections. Unco-ordinated organisation of the Catholic vote took place in several constituencies at the general election of 1807 (64), but by 1823 it had been powerfully augmented by Daniel O'Connell's Catholic Association. It was this body—led by the Catholic middle class and dependent upon the support of the Catholic tenantry—that inspired the defeat of traditional electoral interests in several constituencies at the general election of 1826 (65), and achieved the election of O'Connell for Co. Clare in 1828. It was, in turn, this event which forced the British government to propose a measure of Catholic emancipation in 1829.

As far as procedure and practice are concerned, Irish elections were similar to those in England. Canvassing was common, although the advice tendered by the Rev. Mark Cassidy to the Marquis of Londonderry in 1825 for cultivating the Down gentry (66) would have been unusual. Down had a more numerous gentry than most other Irish counties, where canvassing depended less upon the personal touch and more upon a careful scrutiny of the registration books, and a complicated but very full assessment of the tenant strength of individual landlords (67). In this respect canvassing was of a more detached character than was the case in England.

There were other differences. Until 1820, for example, elections could last for as long as there were freeholders to poll; and, as an accompaniment to this odd state of affairs, there was a stronger tradition of violence and tumult. In most respects, however, there was little difference and the scenes surrounding Montagu Mathew's oration in 1812 would have been as unremarkable in Chelmsford as they were in Clonmel (69).

Borough elections

Before the Union, 117 boroughs returned 236 members to the Irish Parliament and it has been calculated that 223 of these were for seats controlled outright by one or two individuals. This prevalence of 'close' boroughs had much to do with the existence of sixty corporation boroughs with small electorates of about a dozen or so, and the general situation is reflected in the very low total borough electorate of some 14,000. The Act of Union swept away all except thirty-three boroughs; but, even though they were exempted on the basis of their importance in terms of population and wealth, they still provide a miniature reflexion of the system that prevailed during the life of the Irish Parliament. Each type of borough represented before the Union was, for example, represented after it, and for that reason documents for the post-Union period have been selected.

The most open constituencies were eight county boroughs, where the vote belonged to the freemen of the corporation and the 40s freeholders. Electorates in these constituencies were sizeable (about 500 or more) and elections were similar to those in the English freemen boroughs. Each one was stalked by a nearby landlord, who had to exercise both his 'natural interest' arising out of property as well as a careful consideration of the variety of other interests that flourished (70). Seven of the eight boroughs, for example, contained predominantly Catholic populations and, although the corporations and freemen were usually Protestant, Catholics built up sizeable interests amongst the freeholder element. Furthermore, all eight were ports with sizeable numbers of customs and excise officials, which gave the

Irish administration a direct interest in them (71). Finally, they were the most important towns and cities in Ireland, and included Dublin and Cork. Economic, social and political considerations could therefore be of importance in elections (72) and it is significant that, as elsewhere, the Catholic question played an increasingly important part in their outcome.

The remaining boroughs were either firmly controlled by patrons or were subject to venal and violent elections. There were twenty corporation boroughs: in eleven the governing body or council and a select body of freemen could vote; in nine, as in Enniskillen (73), the vote was restricted merely to the council. All were under the control of a nearby landlord.

There were three 'potwalloper' boroughs where £5 householders voted; one 'manor' borough (Mallow in Cork) where the vote was possessed by the 40s freeholders; and finally Dungarvan in Waterford where both £5 householders and 40s freeholders voted. In all five boroughs there were powerful proprietorial interests, although only two were in any sense 'close'. The reason for this was that electorates were sizeable enough to make venality an important feature and, as in Mallow (74), to give the Catholic voters a chance to make themselves felt.

Lastly, there was Trinity College, Dublin, and as one might expect from a university constituency it was, in its customs and predilections, unique (75).

Section one: THE ELECTORAL RESOURCES OF THE MAJOR LANDLORDS AND AN INDICATION OF HOW THEY WERE USED

56 Creating 'fictitious' freeholders. Co. Cork, 1790

Pop c 450,000 and an electorate of c 3,000. The contestants at the general election in that year represented the major interests in the county. They were James Bernard; Lord Kingsborough (the Earl of Kingston's son); and Abraham Morris, who was supported by the writer of this letter, the Earl of Shannon. Bernard and Kingsborough were returned.

Lord Shannon to his son, Henry Boyle, received 9 June 1790
As to this county election it is going on still, to the disgrace of
the H(igh) Sheriff, Ld. Kings (boroug)h & all his party & there
is no saying where it will end & yet all K(ingsboroug)h good
votes having for some time passed been exhausted we are at a
loss every morn(ing) how he will be able to make out the day's
poll. He does not now produce one real voter in 20 & while
Morris polls none but respectable freeholders who are well
known in the face of the county & can not be questioned, he
supports himself by the most infamous perjured, (treacherous)
set of villains that can be conceived; fellows so low as labourers,
torydhers* etc in rags & lice polled against gentlemen of
property & character & he will persist in this, whilst he can get
a Guinea or a man but whilst he has the former he cannot, its
shameful to say, want the latter. Morris is still full handed &
we have got some of K's bucks† in jail for perjury—he is
distress'd & distracted, his looks & conduct shew it & he has
lost his temper. NLI Shannon MSS 13303 (2) 209.

(ii) Although the following document refers to the 40s freeholders who voted in Cork City elections, I have felt it
reasonable to include it here as reliable first-hand evidence
of making freeholders is rare, and because what is described
could equally well apply to county voters.

*William Waggett (Recorder of Cork) to Robert Peel (Chief Secretary to
the Irish Administration)*

23 February 1816
As I perceive from the reports of the proceedings of the House
of Commons, that you have moved for a return of the registries
of Freeholds, I take the liberty of suggesting to you, one or two
matters which appear to me to be defects in our Election Laws.
The facility which is afforded to the making of £20 and 40s

* A version of the Irish word *toiridhe* meaning a wanderer
† Fictitious freeholders

voters is generally complained of. You will find by the return
from this City, how active the exertions have been here. Some
hundreds have been registered since the last election—and on
every occasion, a Roman Catholic Priest attended the Batch,
frequently *explaining* the oath to the ignorant creatures whom
he brought forward.

As the Law now stands, the Lease, or article of agreement,
must be exhibited at the time of registering. It seems however
that the document need not be stamped. At least such is the
opinion of a very eminent lawyer, Serjeant Joy, who was consulted in consequence of a doubt stated by me when sitting at
the Sessions. He said, that as the instrument was not given in
Evidence, it did not come within the provision of the Stamp Act.
His reason for making this objection was this. I observed many
poor wretches brought up to register 40s freeholds, producing
agreements written *just* before, the ink quite moist, and the
paper actually caught up in the hurry in the office of our court.
This seemed to me to be so indecent a practice that I thought
it right to throw any difficulty in the way of it. I have seen men
swear to £20 freeholds, and of course to ye yearly value, who
confessed that they had never seen the premises out of which
ye rent was to arise. . .

Another mischief of a different kind is this. Persons possessed of
estates for long terms of *years* grant leases for *lives* under which it
frequently happens, that a mere leaseholder, who has not a vote
himself, sends in numerous tenantry of *freeholders,* as they swear
themselves to be. These votes I presume would be rejected in a
petition. Our practice offers no other mode of rejection—we
have no security farther than the elector's oath. As to a petition
few candidates venture on it—it is too expensive an experiment.
BM Add. MS 40253 f 40.

57 A landlord's interest in Co. Down, 1812

Pop c 325,000 and an electorate of 14,623. This document
estimates the Marquis of Downshire's personal freeholder
interest and those of his supporters. He contested the county

elections against the Marquis of Londonderry who possessed
about half the Downshire strength.

Lord Downshire	3,763 (freeholders)
Lady Clanwilliam	945
Lord Dungannon	361
F(rancis) Savage	434
Rev. H. Montgomery	292
Mr. Delacherois	164
Lord Bangor and Hon. E. Ward	160
Mr. Isaac	68
Miss Maxwell	20
Mr. McNeil	90
Messrs. Keown and Trotter	44
Rev. W. Hutchinson	53
Rev. H. Waring	34
Chichester Fortescue	43
Mr. Stothard	20
Mr. Waddle	44
Mr. E. Wakefield	45
Mr. J. Maggitt	17
Mr. E. Pottinger	26
Mr. J. Reilly	84
Lord Roden	37
Mr. R. Hall	63
Mr. R. Ross	60
Mr. G. Matthews	37
Lord H. Fitzgerald	25
Mr. J. Hamilton	16
Dean Annesley	27
(in the) borough of Downpatrick	46
	7,018

PRO NI, Downshire MSS D654/A3/1D.

58 Landlords decide the result of an election. Co. Longford, 1807

Pop c 100,000 and an electorate of c 2,000. Edward Wakefield, in his book *An account of Ireland, statistical and political* (1812), wrote of county elections there, 'The Oxmantown estate (that of the earls of Rosse) returns one member; the election of the other is liable to be contested between Sir Thomas Newcomen and the Earl of Granard. Lord Longford has large property in this county, but does not attempt to exercise any political influence.' He nominated the Earl of Rosse and the Earl of Granard as 'patrons' of the constituency. The sitting members at the general election of 1807 were Sir Thomas Fetherston and Lord Granard's son, Lord Forbes. As Lord Forbes was a whig, the Duke of Portland's government hoped for his defeat and the following correspondence took place as a result of that desire.

Sir Arthur Wellesley (Chief Secretary to the Irish administration) to Charles Long in London   28 April 1807

Newcomen will start for Longford, for which county I imagine that Sir Thomas Fetherston must withdraw. If we could prevail upon Lord Longford to start his brother for that county with Newcomen, we should beat out Lord Forbes. *The Duke of Wellington's Supplementary Despatches*, vol 5, 18.

Wellesley subsequently wrote to Lord Rosse about the matter and Rosse replied on 4 May:

I have just communicated your wishes with respect to Longford to the Dowager Lady Rosse, who has the whole arrangement of the property—and she desires me to assure you that she has the best possible wishes for the present Administration, but that an agreement had taken place between the late Lord Rosse and Lord Granard, which she finds herself bound by every tie of affection and respect to fulfil to the utmost of her power—and therefore she must make use of every means she possesses to support Sir Thomas Fetherston and Lord Forbes.

Apsley House MSS.

Wellesley also applied to Lord Longford but to no avail. Fetherston and Forbes were therefore re-elected.

F

Section two: INDEPENDENT INTERESTS IN THE COUNTIES

59 A Handbill in Co. Wexford, 1790

Pop c 110,000 and an electorate of under 1,000. In this handbill two candidates challenge the influence of property as the decisive factor in county elections by deferring to the electors' wishes and listing specific reforms they intend to pursue. They were both unsuccessful at the election.

We do hereby solemnly pledge ourselves, that if we shall have the Honour of being chosen Representatives of the County of Wexford, in the ensuing Parliament, we will cheerfully obey the instructions of our Constituents, whenever they shall favour us with them; and that we will zealously endeavour to procure a Pension Bill, a Place Bill, a Bill to repeal the Dublin Police Bill, and to restrain the arbitrary extent of the County Police, now depending on the Will of the Minister; a Bill to disqualify certain descriptions of persons dependent on Government, from voting for Members to serve in Parliament; a Bill for rendering the Ministers of the Crown responsible: and that we will support every measure likely to do away the late unnecessary charges on the Establishment; that we will strenuously endeavour to procure a Law for the better security of the Liberty of the Press, and the personal Freedom of the Subject.

Dated this 26th day of April, 1790. As candidates of this County of Wexford, *Cornelius Grogan, Frederick Flood.*

Historical Manuscripts Commission, The Dropmore Papers, 1, 578.

---

60 Resolutions of independent freeholders in Co. Wicklow, 1790

Pop c 75,000 and an electorate of c 1,000. Earl Fitzwilliam possessed the strongest proprietary interest in the county. At this election he initially supported William Hume and was thought to be neutral as between the other candidates, the Hon Benjamin Stratford and Nicholas Westby. Hume and

Westby, however, coalesced and defeated Stratford. A number of freeholders took the matter up after the election and sent Stratford the following letter.

————

10th May, 1790

Sir,

The Committee appointed to conduct the Petition to Parliament, complaining of an undue Election and Return for the County of Wicklow, beg leave to send you the following, and to request such assistance as you may think fit to give . . .

————

At a meeting of a Number of Independent Freeholders of the County of Wicklow, Captain Saunders, in the Chair

The following Resolutions were unanimously agreed to:

1st. Resolved. That it is the opinion of this meeting, that the independence of this county, and the freedom of election, were materially injured by certain proceedings during the late election of members to serve in Parliament.

2ndly. Resolved. That where three candidates, stand for a county, it is very possible, by an artful coalition at the time of polling, (of two against one) for those who otherwise would be the last on the poll, if such stood singly, to throw out the candidate possessed of the hearts and greater number of voters, as was the fact at the last election for this county; and that such conduct ought to be discountenanced.

3rdly. Resolved. That it appears by the poll taken at the last election for this county, that 400 single votes were polled for Mr. Stratford, but 52 for Mr. Hume, and but 13 for Mr. Westby, and that had Mr. Stratford joined with either of them and had their second votes, he not only must have been first on the poll, but have brought in which ever of the other candidates he chose to have taken by the hand.

4thly. Resolved. That it appears to us, that notwithstanding the said coalition of Mr. Westby and Mr. Hume, the majority which occasioned their return, was obtained by very indirect means, of which there is sufficient evidence.

5thly. Resolved. That a Petition be presented to the House of Commons on the part of those electors who maintained the independence of this county, and freedom of election in the person of the Hon. John Stratford, complaining of an undue election and return for said county.

6thly. Resolved. That a Committee be appointed for carrying the purposes of this meeting into execution, and that they do request the co-operation of their fellow freeholders throughout this extensive county, embarked in the same cause, in pursuing such vigorous and constitutional measures as are most likely to remedy the grievance they labour under from the late return, and better maintenance of our mutual rights and privileges.

7thly. Resolved. That prosecutions for perjury and suborna-tion of perjury and bribery, be forthwith carried on against those on whom such attrocious acts can be proved.

8thly. Resolved. That said Committees are hereby requested to receive all information of illicit and illegal practices respect-ing said election, and carrying on said prosecutions.

9thly. Resolved. That the following Address be presented to the Hon. John Stratford, our legal Representative, and that these Resolutions, Address, and his answer, be inserted in the public prints. Sheffield City Library, Wentworth Woodhouse Muniments F 93/45.

_____

Section three: GOVERNMENT INTERESTS IN THE COUNTIES

61 Crown property in Co. Wexford, 1818

Pop c 170,000 and an electorate of c 7,500. The Marquis of Ely, the Earl of Mountnorris, Sir Frederick Flood, Lord Courtown and the Alcock, Carew, Colclough and Ram families had the strongest interests. At the general election in 1818, Robert Shapland Carew and Caesar Colclough were returned with only forty-six votes between Colclough and the third candidate.

Lord Courtown to Robert Peel (Irish Chief Secretary)

Courtown, Co. Wexford

June 24th 1818

There is a hill near Wexford called the Mountain of Forth, which belongs to the Crown, and on which there reside about 180 families, who pay no rent to any one, and who have all small holdings, sufficient to entitle them to vote. Being all Roman Catholics they have always gone with the party that espoused that cause. They are always in dread that the Government may have it surveyed, and claim it was their right. Now if you could send somebody down there, only to look at it, and to enquire into the nature of their holdings etc. as if from the Government, it might possibly secure these 180 men (no small number in a contested election) to vote for Lords Valentia and Stopford. They have now, as they always do, promised to vote for all the candidates, but they certainly will go with Messrs. Carew and Colclough, unless some steps of this sort are taken. Our election begins on Monday next the 29th. BM Add. MS 40278 f 229.

62 Some votes made available to government in Co. Galway, 1820

Pop c 165,000 and an electorate of c 13,000. Gregory, an under-secretary in the Irish administration, did not stand and the sitting members were re-elected.

P. Waldron to William Gregory

Longford, 18th Feb.y 1820

Having seen in the Freeman's Journal your intention of being a candidate for the County of Galway, I hold a farm of about 75 acres of the Glynske estate under Sir John Burke, to whom I am not in any way bound to vote with, and on which I have register.d 12 freeholders, tho not having the pleasure of knowing you personally, I shall feel happy in giving you any support in my power at the ensuing election or any other time—I have

written to your office frequently, wishing to know if there was
any application from my relative, *my Lord Castlereagh*, in my
favour—I never had the honour of an answer. Dublin SPO
576/512/2.

63 Government patronage in Westmeath, 1818–20

An extract from the chief secretary's memorandum book for
1818 which itemises the details of government patronage and
the holders of county honours. Pakenham and Rochfort
were the county MPs.

Westmeath County

(1) Lieut. Colonel the Hon. H. Pakenham (Government) Lord
Longford [Pakenham's father] is a Representative Peer; is
Custos Rotulorum of the County; is a Trustee of the Linen
Board. He is brother-in-law of the Duke of Wellington. His
brother, Admiral Thomas Pakenham has £1200 compensation
as Master General of the Ordnance granted at time of Union.
His son Thomas £100 per annum as Secretary to ditto, and his
son William £50 per annum as Clerk to ditto—children at the
time. (2) Gustavus Rochfort. (Government). Has a hundred
and fifty objects with Government. His son Richard has lately
been removed from an office at Drogheda to a better one in
Dublin.

Distribution of honours

Governors: Lord Castlemain, Earl of Westmeath and Gustavus
    Rochfort
Custos Rotulorum: Earl of Longford
Colonel of Militia—Earl of Westmeath
    BM Add. MS 40298 ff 42–3.

Section four: THE CATHOLIC VOTE IN COUNTY ELECTIONS

64 Co. Limerick, 1807

Pop c 250,000 and an electorate of c 7,000. Some eight

families had strong proprietary interests in this predominantly Catholic county.

W. T. Monsell to John Foster (Irish Chancellor of the Exchequer)
Limerick, 23 May 1807

As a friend to the Protestant Establishment and to the present Administration, I take the liberty of applying to you, respecting the present contest for the County of Limerick—Mr. Quin, the candidate to whom I am opposed is an avowed partisan of the late Ministers, and is also I understand under positive engagements to the Roman Catholics. I applied for the assistance of His Majesty's servants here, with a promise to support them should they by their assistance forward my election—I received for an answer, 'that I had so little prospect of success, they would not endanger the peace of the county'. I know in other counties they have encouraged contests with much less prospect of success, but I must suppose they took their information respecting this county from Lady Clare or Colonel Odell, whose particular interest it happens to be, to oppose me. Why the real interests of Government should be sacrificed to their private convenience I do not see. The Roman Catholics had a meeting last night and determined to support Mr. Quin and oppose me, to the utmost of their power—in consequence of this, a Roman Catholic tenant of my own told me publicly in the streets of Limerick he could not vote for me, it was as much as his life was worth.'

On 7 June, Monsell reported his defeat at the polls to the government, concluding that he had received the largest number of single votes and that some 100 Roman Catholics were deterred by threats from voting for him. Apsley House MSS.

---

65 Co. Waterford, 1826

Pop c 160,000 and an electorate of c 3,000. Elections in this predominantly Catholic county had traditionally been controlled by the Dukes of Devonshire and the Marquises of

Waterford—the latter being the heads of the Beresford family, who were associated above all others, in the minds of the Catholics, with the sterner side of the Protestant ascendancy. At the general election in 1826 Lord George Beresford, the brother of the Marquis of Waterford, was beaten into third place by Henry Villiers-Stuart, a liberal Protestant who supported Catholic emancipation and who was here supported by a particularly well organised Catholic vote. Thomas Wyse, the author of the following description, played no small part in that organisation, and he was assisted by the inspiration provided by the Catholic Association as well as by Daniel O'Connell, who acted as Stuart's counsel. However, it was Wyse's view that Stuart's success was due more to local efforts than to the metropolitan guidance of the Association, with which he was at odds at this time. Wyse first describes the activities of the Catholic priests:

The arguments which they used, had no connexion with their spiritual power. They were based on the principles of general morality, and applicable to the rights and duties of all classes of citizens. They neither fulminated excommunications, nor withheld the sacraments as it is averred; but they spoke of the crime of perjury, and of the oath of the freeholder at the hustings, and of the duty of the elector, and of the baseness of bribery; and if such themes made the impression which they ought to have done, it is to the credit of the priest and of the people, and an influence which every good man should obey, and of which every free citizen should be proud.

These instructions of the priest in private were seconded by the earnest co-operation of the agitators in public. Their first care was to provide a proper organisation. The system they adopted for the purpose was simple, but all-powerful. A general committee was established in the county town. It consisted nominally of many members—a few only acted. They had their branch committees in every barony, constituted on a similar principle. The priests were honorary members. In attendance

on these committees were two local agents, who furnished weekly, their reports. The baronial committees made similar reports, to the general committee and received in turn its instructions. Each parish priest, each local agent, and each baronial committee, had their registry book. They were required to make upon each name, besides, the usual remarks relative to the right of voting, etc. their own particular and personal observations. These books were handed in from the several parts of the country a week or two previous to the election, and from this information was compiled an analytic view (which scarcely presented a single error when brought to the test of experience) of the temper and disposition of the entire county. The whole of this machinery was soon in operation, and worked admirably; but it was chiefly calculated to preclude confusion, to restrain and apply the excitement, but not to create the excitement itself. Something more was requisite. It was determined to make an almost individual appeal to the forty-shilling constituency of the county. A certain number of the committee were deputed to address each parish, in rotation. They chose Sunday for these assemblies, to avoid the inconvenience and tumult of specially-convened meetings; and for two months previous to the election, they were to be seen, before the altar of the respective chapels, haranguing the people on the discharge of their approaching duties. Their reasoning was short and simple. They took the 'bribery oath' in one hand, the 'two addresses' of Lord George Beresford in the other. They asked the people, how they could take the money of the Beresfords and that oath at the same time? They asked the old and young, whether their priests had not told them that perjury was a crime? They told them, that the oath which had just been read should be put to every freeholder: they warned them to reflect upon its deep import, and to reflect in due time . . .
The priest then stepped forward, and addressed them, in their own vehement and figurative language. Resolutions were next framed and proposed by priest, gentleman, and farmer, indiscriminately. The next day, they were struck off on small

slips of paper, and on the following Sunday scattered to the amount of thousands in the neighbouring parish, previous to the assembly of the day. Shame and emulation are powerful stimulants. They are particularly so in Ireland, even in those portions of the country which are considered the most abandoned. The 'Crusade', as it was denominated, worked its effect. It was soon a disgrace to be in the minority. Thomas Wyse. *Historical Sketch of the late Catholic Association of Ireland*, 1 (1829), 284–8.

Section five: COUNTY ELECTIONEERING
66 Canvassing the gentry in Co. Down in 1825
See (57) for the general background. With a future election in mind, the Rev Mark Cassidy sent the following advice to the Marquis of Londonderry in February 1825:

... there are so many independent squires and squireens, all of whom, as well as their Wives and daughters, require the nicest management. For the marquis to keep up the interests of his family it would be necessary that he should spend as much of his time here as possible, not only entertain the heads of Houses, but enter into the most familiar intercourse with them, surprise the breakfast table of one in a morning, the dinner of another in an evening, chat with the ladies, view all the imaginary improvements of the house, farmyard, farm etc., and enter into all the domestic concerns of the whole family. Nor will this be sufficient, the marchioness must also devote much of her time and ease to the same purpose; she must enter into the greatest familiarity with them, be personally acquainted with them all, know the Christian names of the daughters, the policies of the families, the taste of the individuals, balance her attentions with the most scrupulous exactness, so as not to hurt the feelings of one by a greater attention to another, and in all cases appear to think that she is both honoured and gratified by their company in place of appearing to think herself superior. PRO NI, Cassidy MSS, D 1088/45.

67 Results of a completed canvass in Co. Wexford, 15 June 1817

Pop c 170,000 and an electorate of c 7,500. The candidates at the general election in 1818 were Lords Valentia and Stopford, who were supported by the Irish administration and acted together; Robert Shapland Carew, and Caesar Colclough. Despite the prediction of this canvass, Carew and Colclough were returned, although it is fair to add that it was an extremely close contest.

Enclosed by Lord Mountmorris (Valentia's father) to Robert Peel (Irish Chief Secretary), 30 June 1817

| Barony's | Total of Barony | Certain Votes | | | | Probable Votes | | | | Doubtful |
		Lord Valentia	Lord Stopford	Carew	Colclough	Lord Valentia	Lord Stopford	Carew	Colclough	
Bantry	1,738	557	548	1,011	1,032	62	28	47	22	146
Ballaghkeene	1,191	895	833	121	100	93	37	109	55	121
Bargy	485	75	73	291	286	11	11	14	20	177
Forth	448	132	124	214	216	15	16	7	9	163
Gorey	843	596	602	217	220	13	9	2	2	24
Scarawalsh	1,176	721	732	298	350	75	38	47	22	23
Shelmalier	785	306	299	331	330	23	16	19	19	222
Shelburn	894	370	351	519	500	1	1	14	14	18
	7,560	3,652	3,562	3,002	3,034	293	156	259	163	894

Clergy mostly with the Lords but numbers unknown, probably above 30—but the registry of 14th June 1817 is not included in the above on which Colclough and Carew have a majority of from 30 to 40.—We had a majority of 60 on the registry of the 16th June 1817 which is one day too late.

	Lord V.	Lord S.	Carew	Colclough	Doubtfuls	
Certain Votes	3,652	3,562	3,002	3,034	894	doubled
Probables	293	156	259	163		single
	3,945	3,718	3,261	3,197	448	

Giving a majority to Lord V. over Lord S. of 227
,,   ,,   over Mr. Carew of 684
,,   ,,   over Mr. Colclough of 748

BM Add. MS 40278 f 311.

68 Polling in Co. Down, 1790

An extract from Lord Hillsborough's 'check book' on the poll (*opposite page*), shows how a candidate's tenantry were usually registered together and that they voted in identical ways. In this case the Clanwilliam tenants voted (with two exceptions) for S (Robert Stewart, later Lord Castlereagh) and W (The Hon Robert Ward), and Annesley's and Ogle's tenants for H (Lord Hillsborough) and M (Capt George Matthews). It also shows how a check was kept on the legality of qualifications as in the case of voter 826, Samuel Bell.

See document extract on page 173.
PRO NI, Downshire MSS D 654/A3/1B.

69 A poll in progress for Tipperary, 1812

Pop c 350,000 and an electorate of c 18,000. Montagu Mathew and Francis Prittie were returned after a hot contest, the poll taking place at Clonmel.

The Times reported: The mornings at Clonmel afford such displays of popular eloquence, as, perhaps have never been paralleled in the British Empire, whether in matter, manner or occasion. About eleven o'clock the streets are thronged with freeholders, the Court and booths crowded, the partisans anxious, the examining agents clamorous, and the din of oaths, questions, wrangles, interruptions, shouts, etc., resounding even to the opposite banks of the River Suir. Suddenly the sound of

No.	Electors Names	Abodes	Free-holds	Landlords	Date of Registry	H	M	S	W	date of voting Objections, Disqualifications
821	Bigham Archibald	Killysavan	40s.	Lord Clan-william	26 Jan 1789	0	0	1	1	S.C.* 28th May
822	Bardley Alexander	Derrydrumac	"	"	"	0	0	1	1	D.C.† 27th May
823	Bartley Jonathan	"	"	"	"	0	0	1	1	D.C. 29th June
824	Bell William	Drumlough	"	"	"	0	0	1	1	D.C. 8th May
825	Bell Alexander	"	"	"	"	0	0	1	1	S.C. 8th May
827	Bell James	"	"	"	"	0	0	1	1	D.C. 28th May
826	Bell Samuel	"	"	"	"	0	0	1	1	D.C. 22nd May only 3½ acres at a high rent, his father died lately, made a will and left land to mother and has no title and a minor
828	Beaumont John	Rathfryland	"	"	"	0	0	1	1	D.C. 10th June all the oaths
829	Bradfoot John	"	"	"	"	0	0	1	1	S.C. 8th May
830	Boyd Thomas	"	"	"	"	0	0	1	1	S.C. 10th June
831	Boyd John Jun.	"	"	"	"	0	0	1	1	S.C. 10th June
832	Blakely James	"	"	"	"	1	1	0	0	S.C. 6th May
833	Bermison Joseph	Lissize	"	Lord Annesley	"	1	1	0	0	S.C. 5th June
834	Baillie James	Newcastle	"	"	"	1	1	0	0	D.C. 14th June
835	Baillie Robert	"	"	"	"	1	1	0	0	S.C. 14th June
836	Berry Thomas	"	"	"	"	1	1	0	0	S.C. 14th June
837	Berry Charles	"	"	"	"	1	1	0	0	S.C. 14th January
838	Bell James	Derryneale	"	Mr. Ogle	"	1	1	0	0	S.C. 17th May
839	Burden Samuel	"	"	"	"	1	1	0	0	D.C. 24th May
840	Bell Henry	"	"	"	"	1	1	0	0	D.C. 18th May

* S(heriff's) C(ourt). † D(eputy) C(ourt)

carriages is heard, the cries of thousands follow: several hundreds of men, women, and boys are seen to run at full speed to the great place in front of the inns and hotels, followed by a grand and imposing procession of coaches, chaises, and various vehicles, bearing freeholders in the interest of Mathew and Prittie, from the distant parts of this extensive county. Each coach is decorated with boughs of oak, sycamore, etc., the heads of all the horses are similarly adorned. Bugles and French horns are sounded by the outside passengers. Thus, about 100 men enter the town each morning by the Cashel road, followed by about 200 horsemen and 500 pedestrians. Arrived at this destination, the entire force comes to a great halt. All the windows are stuck thick with company, elegant ladies, fashionable youths . . . In the midst of this scene General Mathew comes forth, mounts the very summit of the largest coach, waves his hand, and becomes uncovered. Instantly, the music ceases, the din is hushed . . . The General from his lofty rostrum, sends forth stentorian notes to the wondering populace . . . *The Times* (13 November 1812).

Section six: ELECTIONS IN COUNTY-BOROUGH CONSTITUENCIES

70 Proprietorial and independent interests in Limerick city, 1812 and 1818

Pop c 60,000 and an electorate of between 600 and 1,000 freemen and freeholders. Limerick was the third largest city in Ireland with a predominantly Catholic population and a prosperity based upon woollen and cattle exports. The issue at elections was that Charles Vereker (later Lord Gort) had the strongest interest in the corporation, while Lord Limerick and his son, Lord Glentworth, looked for their strength from their property in the constituency, and amongst the Catholic and freeholder interests. At the 1812 election, Glentworth unsuccessfully challenged Vereker and was supported by the 'Friends of Independence' (a). In 1818 Lord Limerick was still trying to regain his old influence and, although he clearly felt he had a natural interest (b), his candidate was again beaten by a Vereker.

___

(a) *Friends of Independence*

AT a General Meeting of the FRIENDS to the INDEPENDENCE of LIMERICK, held at Commercial Buildings on Monday, the 24th August 1812, Lord Viscount Glentworth in the chair, the following resolutions, moved by JOHN TUTHILL Esq., and seconded by JOHN HOWLEY Esq., were unanimously adopted; RESOLVED—That we deem it necessary to hold frequent Meetings of the Friends to the independence of Limerick

—That the object of the Friends of Independence is confined to the following Purposes

1st The ascertaining and enforcing by legal means the Rights, Liberties, Privileges, Immunities and Franchises of the City of Limerick

2dly The procuring, according to CHARTER and rights of that City, the perfect freedom of election of all the officers of the Corporation and of its Representatives in Parliament

3dly Of ascertaining the Legal Revenues of the City of Limerick, and causing the same to be duly accounted for, and expended in the manner most useful to the City and its Inhabitants

RESOLVED—That the Friends of Independence are enemies equally to every distinction of Party, and to every Species of Monopoly; and they solemnly pledge themselves never to desist until the object they have in view, and which they have so explicitly stated should be fully attained. *The Dublin Correspondent* (15 August 1812)

(b) *Lord Limerick to Robert Peel (Chief Secretary to the Irish administration)*

South Hill Park, Bracknell, Berks, 23 Oct. 1817
The reason however that I trouble you with this letter, is not for the purpose of further urging Mr Baylee's pretensions to a promotion, which he has so richly deserved, but merely to endeavour to set myself right in your opinion & to show that I

had not asked for a situation, which my former & present interest in Limerick did not fully entitle me to look to.

I shall not weary you by stating by what manoeuvres & breach of confidence in persons *now dead*, my family lost its commanding interest in the Corporation.

It is necessary however that you should know that notwithstanding the manoeuvre alluded to, which was the influence of my Family, that I was always returned to Parliament for the City of Limerick without opposition, as long as I remained a Commoner. Nay more previous to the Union I returned a member for the City, who was not even possess'd of a vote there . . . I trust however that I shall not be considered as in opposition to Government by endeavouring to regain an influence of which I was long possessed in a City, where I have more Property, than the whole of the Ancient and Loyal Corporation. BM Add. MS 40271 f 77.   ———

71 Government interests in these constituencies

(i) Drogheda, 1802; pop c 15,000 and an electorate of c 450: the freemen of the corporation and the 40s freeholders in the borough possessed the franchise. Bribery and corruption were common features of elections and at this election the absurd situation emerged of the Irish administration campaigning for one candidate—Henry Meade Ogle —while the British government supported the other— Edward Hardman—who in fact won by five votes. This document lists the voters connected with the Irish administration, their occupations and places of residence.

Ardsall Nichs Esqre	Army
Atkinson Wm. [in the] Revenue	Auchnacloy
Brabazon Lambert Esqre.	Cavendish Row [Dublin]
Burgh Thomas Esqre.	Ordnance, Sackville Street [Dublin]
Caldwell John [a] Guager	Drogheda
Coote Sir Eyre	Major General
Courtney Alexr.	Ordnance Yard
Corry James Esqre.	Linen Hall
Dundas Col. Thos.	. . . .

Edwards James Esqre.	Surveyor General
Edwards John Esqre.	Custom House, Dublin
Finch Honble. Major Genl.	Quarters
Hawthorn John	Custom House [Dublin]
Huey Spencer Esqre.	Landwaiter, Drogheda
Kaine Willm.	Revenue, Drogheda
Kaine George	Revenue, Narrow Water [Co. Down]
Kirwan Revd. Dean	....
Lees John Esqre.	Post Office, Dublin
McCartney John	Revenue at Doughertys, Townsend St. [Dublin]
McCartney John Junr.	Brittain Street, Hairdresser
McGuiness Captn. Richard	....
Moore Thos.	Revenue, Rostrevor [Co. Down]
Moylan Rt. Revd. Frans.	R[oma]n Cath. B[isho]p of Cork
Perry Edward	Revenue, Lowr. Dorset St. [Dublin]
Pollock John Esqre. Attey.	Jervis Street [Dublin]
Riddock Wilcocks	Revenue [Dublin]
Ronan Geo. David	Wicklow
Sherrard Thos.	Wide Steer Surveyor, Dublin
Smyth Benjm.	Revenue, Drogheda
Wilmot Edward	Revenue, Cork
Wynne John	Revenue, Drogheda
Wynne Charles	Revenue, Armagh
Jones Lancelot	Coast Office, Drogheda
Richardson John	Revenue, Dunleary [Dublin]
Foster Jno. Wm. Esqure.	Collector, Drogheda
McEntegart George	Post Master, Drogheda
Taylor Thomas	Work House, Dublin
Head Danial	Ordnance Office
Holmes Wm.	Stamp Office, Drogheda
Warburton Thos.	Revenue, Bannagher
Cuthbert Eccles Esqre.	son in law of Mr. Wilde of the Custom House, Dublin
Collins Thomas	Is Deputy in Drogheda to Mr. Robt. Cosgrave, Customer & Comptroller of Dundalk & Drogheda
Collins	Son of Thomas Collins
Morris Henry	Simpsons Hospital [Dublin]—Mr. Robt. Duy the Secry. could obtain this mans vote or keep him in town.

Dublin SPO, 521/131/8.

(ii) Waterford, 1802; pop c 25,000 and an electorate of
c 1,000: the freemen of the corporation and the 40s freeholders of the borough possessed the franchise. In this
case the Irish administration fails to secure a vote for their
candidate, Sir John Newport who was beaten in the poll
by William Alcock.

Joseph Greene to Alexander Marsden (a secretary in the Irish
administration)   Waterford, 18 June 1802

It having been communicated to me by Mr. May, Collector
of this Port, that the wish of the present Government of this
country, is to support Sir John Newport, in his political views
on the ensuing election as representative for this city: thus being
called upon, as a servant of the Crown, to support these views, I
find myself justifiable in troubling you with a few observations.
The late Lord Waterford and my family were engag'd in a
political conflict for a series of years; and until the late Lord
Lieutenant of this part of the United Kingdom, (my ever most
revered, esteemed, and honourable friend), healed the wounds
which did subsist between our families; and in consideration of
Lord Waterford's handsome conduct to me on that occasion; in
return, my brother and myself promised him our political
support unequivocally in this country: and as the late Lord
Waterford had been uniform in his support of Government, and
countenanc'd of course by the Administration thereof, I had
not any cause to suspect that the present Marquis of Waterford
would, & so immediately too, after the decease of his father,
have given cause to sacrifice such protection; therefore, the
cement which did take place between the late Marquis and my
family, has been renewed between his successor, my brother,
and myself; I am therefore under honourable engagements to
support his Lordships friend on the next election to be held for
this city. The statement I have made, I trust will fully plead my
excuse with Government, for my line of conduct; at the same
time allow me to declare, that few men would be more happy
to meet the views of Government which you will have the

goodness to communicate accordingly. Dublin SPO, 620/62/
11.

_____

72 Some leading questions to the candidates at the Dublin City election of 1818

Pop c 170,000 and an electorate of about 1,800. The exclusively Protestant Dublin Corporation entirely dominated
city elections, there being very few freeholders. Parliamentary
elections were in fact corporation elections and, as the corporation was representative of the leading commercial and
social interests in the city, candidates were selected on the
basis of their being worthy to represent them. As a consequence there was a tradition of vetting candidates and in this
case the Guild of Glovers puts the following questions to
Henry Grattan and Robert Shaw to satisfy itself of their
suitability as MPs.

_____

Mr Willis, as representative of the Corporation of Glovers,
put three questions to the candidates:
  1. Whether they would use their best exertions to procure
total repeal of the window tax?
  2. Whether they would endeavour to bring about a repeal, or
at least a revision of the Act of Union?
  3. Whether they would support any measure which may be
brought forward for limiting the duration of Parliaments?
. . .
  Mr Shaw next came forward, and was warmly received. He
addressed the meeting to the following effect: 'Mr Sheriff and
Gentlemen, I now, for the fifth time, offer myself to you to
represent this great City in Parliament. Four times I have been
fortunate enough to receive your approbation, and certainly, a
fifth proof of your confidence will not lessen my desire or my
exertions to serve you. I am, as my respected friend who
seconded me, observed, wholly unfettered by party connexions
of any kind, and I always support such measures as I think
most calculated to serve my country, and the City of Dublin,

especially. With respect to the first of the questions which have been proposed to my Right Honorable Friend and myself, I trust I may firstly refer you to my past conduct on the subject of the Window Tax. I shall only say now, that my exertions to procure the relief you require, shall not be less zealous than they have been.

To that question which regards the Union, I may say with my Right Hon. Colleague, that that measure had no more sincere opponent than myself. I did not give it the same opposition which he did, because I did not possess the same talents, but such humble abilities as I could command were strenuously exerted against it. I now consider a repeal of that destructive measure as hopeless and almost impossible; if it were otherwise, nothing could give me more true pleasure than the prospect of being an instrument in effecting so desirable an object.

With respect to the duration of Parliament, there have been so many plans of reform presented to the public, that it really requires much consideration to enable an honest man to make up his mind upon their various merits and defects. The scheme of universal suffrage and annual Parliaments seems now to have lost all chance of succeeding; but a limitation of the duration of Parliament would be, I think, a salutary measure.

I have only now to repeat, that I hope my public conduct has merited your approval. If I have erred, the fault has been of the head, not of the heart. We cannot command success, but I have endeavoured to deserve approbation (Loud applause).

The last pronouncements were now made, and the Sheriff declared Mr Grattan and Mr Shaw duly elected. These Gentlemen returned thanks. *The Dublin Correspondent* (1 July 1818) reporting events of the previous day.

Section seven: A 'CLOSE' CORPORATION BOROUGH
73 Enniskillen

A 'close' corporation borough which survived the Union and which in 1831 had a population of c 5,000 and an electorate of fifteen—all members of the corporation. The following are

items 57 and 58 of the official inquiry into the affairs of the
corporation, published in 1836, which reflect accurately the
general situation in the constituency during this period.

---

57. The corporation is under the Patronage of the Earl of
Enniskillen, whose influence in it is paramount. All the
members are nominated by him, or at his instance. The
following will show the members of the corporation, and
their connexion with Lord Enniskillen, at the time of the
holding of our enquiry.

   1. The Earl of Enniskillen
   2. Lord Cole, the patron's son
   3. Arthur Henry Cole, the patron's brother
   4. Richard Magennis, the patron's nephew
   5. William Gabbett, connected by marriage with the
      patron
   6. Hamilton Irvin, a friend of the patron, major in the
      militia regiment of which the patron is colonel
   7. William Corry, adjutant of the patron's regiment
   8. Baptist Gamble Swift, M.D., assistant surgeon of the
      patron's regiment
   9. Charles Ovendon M.D., the patron's family physician
   10. Adam Nixon, a friend of the patron, and clerk of the
      peace for the county, of which the patron is custos
      rotolorum
   11. Joseph Maguire, a land agent of the patron
   12. Rev. James Fox, a friend of the patron
   13. Rev. James Rogers, the like
   14. Rev. Abraham Hamilton, the like
   15. Richard Deane, the like.

58. Of these 15 members comprising the governing body, only
four, ..., were resident in the town at the time of our
enquiry. Several of the others lived at distances varying
from one to seven miles from the town. .... It was
stated to us, by members of the corporation, to be the
invariable practice to ascertain, upon any change of

G

members, Lord Enniskillen's wishes respecting a new appointment, and to elect at his nomination. Municipal Corporation Report (1836) vol 24, 1085.

___

Section eight: THE CATHOLIC VOTE IN A 'MANOR' BOROUGH

74 Mallow, Co. Cork, in 1818

Pop c 7,000 and an electorate of c 500: the 40s freeholders in the manor of Mallow possessed the franchise. A number of landlords had ambitions in Mallow, but by 1818 the vital electoral interest belonged to the Catholic voters. Their declaration at this election in favour of William Becher forced the other candidate, Sir James Cotter, to decline a contest. Becher was therefore returned.

___

(a) *An address to the constituency.*

To THE GENTLEMEN, CLERGY, AND FREEHOLDERS OF THE BOROUGH OF MALLOW.

GENTLEMEN,

A CONSIDERABLE time has elapsed since I took the liberty of addressing you, and declaring my intention to become a Candidate for the honour of Representing you in Parliament, whenever a vacancy should occur. That opportunity to which I have so anxiously looked forward, has at length arrived; a Dissolution of Parliament has taken place, and I now beg leave most earnestly to solicit the honour of your Votes and Interest at the ensuing Election. It is, I hope, unnecessary to assure you of my stedfast adherence to the principles which I have already professed, and that if it shall please you to confide to my care the important duties of your Representative, I shall endeavour to discharge the trust with Independence and Integrity.

Ballygiblin, 18 June 1818.   William Becher

(b) *A newspaper report*

'At a very numerous Meeting of the Roman Catholics of the

Borough of Mallow, held at the Assembly Rooms, on Friday, the 19th inst. pursuant to Public Notice, Mr. OWEN MADDEN in the chair.

The following Resolutions were unanimously agreed to

RESOLVED—That we entirely confide in and approve of the political principles avowed by our favourite Candidate for the Borough, William Wrixon Becher, Esq. that we believe his opinions and wishes on the subject (Catholic emancipation), most interesting to us as fellow subjects and citizens, are the result of his mature and sincere conviction, and not a recent adoption of sentiments to gain the support of our Body at the approaching election.

RESOLVED—Therefore that we will steadily support and most earnestly recommend the Independent Electors of the Borough to rally round him.

RESOLVED—That we will at all times uphold the Candidate who shall express the wishes of his constituents, and support the independence of this Country in the Legislative Assembly, uninfluenced by party motive or political intrigue.

RESOLVED—That the above Resolutions be printed in the Southern Reporter, Cork Morning Intelligence, Cork Mercantile Chronicle, Advertiser, and Dublin Evening Post.

OWEN MADDEN, Chairman
JOHN BOURKE, Secretary

BM Add. MS 40278 f 243.

Section nine: TRINITY COLLEGE, DUBLIN
75 The 1818 election

Elections at the university sometimes turned on national issues and sometimes, as in this case, on matters of purely domestic interest. The candidates at this election were John Wilson Croker and William Conyngham Plunket, between whom the Irish administration maintained an uneasy neutrality. The Dr Sadleir referred to in this extract gave his vote to Plunket and this secured him the return.

John Wilson Croker to Robert Peel (Chief Secretary to the Irish administration)

16 May, 1818.

I will now endeavour to give you a general view of the state of our case. The election is in the Provost, Fellows, and scholars; 1–25–70—total 96, but minors being excluded, no greater number has, we think, ever voted than 69, so that 35 never was beaten. Of the 70 scholars 1 in 5 change every year, and if the election should take place before the 8th of July, a curious question will arise, for the new fifth will be elected on Monday, yet the outgoing fifth hold their offices till the 7th July. We think that they do so only by courtesy and contrary to law, and that the newcomers are the real electors. This throws a doubt over all our calculations. I shall not be able to tell you till Monday which way it would be for my advantage to have the question decided, but I can state to you the present view of the canvass. Of the outgoers 4 are pledged to me and 3 to Mr. Plunket, and 6 have not yet declared, but will probably be divided between us. He has 4 minors pledged to him and I have the same number. There are 5 other minors all of whom are well inclined to me, except one. These two denominations are I think, 'hors de combat', but of them, I think, I should be sure of the majority. Of the present scholars, omni exceptione majores, I have 15 sure votes, and he has 12, and there are undecided 2 fellows and 13 scholars. So that on the whole I can reckon for him this day but 21 effective votes and for me 28. The incomers, not being yet known, cannot be reckoned upon, but I am assured that I have a *decided majority* of those who are likely to be chosen, and it is thought that their number capable of voting will be about 10, which would make the whole number likely to vote 74, a larger number than ever has voted; so that 37 with the *Provost's casting vote* will carry the election. Now even if I only divide the newcomers with him, I shall have 33, and I have therefore only 4 out of the 15 undecided to procure to ascertain my success. Now I have the fairest prospect of 4 scholars at least out of the 15 which would exactly answer, but as all the scholars votes are liable to questions of minority, and as we cannot be sure of *dividing* the incomers, we ought to spare no efforts to increase our strength. Now, have a little patience while I tell you how this is to be done. Mr. Wray, one of the fellows, is the most wavering and one of the most *interested* men alive; he had promised me, but I believe Plunket has persuaded him that *he* has the Government support, and he has withdrawn his promise and holds his vote in suspense. Dr. Sadleir, another of the fellows, has two scholars his pupils, who will follow him; he was favourable to me, but he had promised the junior fellows to act in the way which might appear most conducive to the repeal of the statue of celibacy, and Mr. Plunket having represented to him that he had exerted himself to settle that point and that he had even procured from the Duke of Cumberland (University Chancellor) his assurance that tho' he was rather inclined to approve the principle of the Statute yet he had no objection to grant *dispensations* to the present 6 unmarried fellows, and that as soon as Lord Sidmouth should return to town, H.R.H. would have this matter carried through. This Dr. Sadleir told me today, and when I assured him that three days after Mr. Plunket's departure I had heard nothing of this from you or any other of the ministers, tho' it was so obvious a topic of intelligence, if you had been aware of it, he expressed great surprise, and stated that he would suspend his vote till the day of the election and then act in the way most likely to further the object of the repeal. BM Add. MS 40184 f 157.

PART FIVE

Some Examples of Extra-Parliamentary Demands for Parliamentary Reform

INTRODUCTION

It would be wrong to think that even a majority of those who advocated parliamentary reform in this period had in mind the achievement of a parliamentary democracy similar to that which was to emerge in Britain during the late nineteenth and early twentieth centuries. Research into the ideological ancestry, social bases and economic ambitions of the various groups that advocated reform in this period suggests a multiplicity of purposes, some of which looked to the past rather than to the future. Democratic thinking was in its formative stages and was hardly capable of evisaging a system which was eventually achieved by hopeful expediency, timely concession, a reverence for well-tried conventions, and a recognition of certain basic civil rights. In other words, parliamentary reform meant different things to different people. It is broadly true that until the late 1780s the demand for parliamentary reform came mainly from those connected with parliament, who sought to restore to the electoral system a purity they believed had been lost by an intolerable increase in corruption and executive and aristocratic 'influence'. They wished, therefore, to reduce the number of 'close' boroughs, and to make elections more 'open' to the gentry and the freeholders. However, in the late 1780s the implications of the French Revolution and the more noticeable social results of the industrial revolution shattered the harmony of the reform movement into discordant elements. To a few, parliamentary reform was now basically a matter of civil rights along the lines of Paine's *Rights of Man*; to others, it was a matter of adjusting the electoral system so that it could represent in some degree the new industrial and commercial interests; to some, it still implied a reduction in the powers of the Crown and its ministers; to yet others, it was a means of enabling certain social groups to achieve specific legislative ambitions. The London Corresponding Society, founded in 1792, reflected this state of fragmentation. It was one of the first reform societies that specifically catered for those hitherto largely excluded from the representative system—the artisans. Furthermore, in seeking to restore the 'genuine spirit of the British Constitution', it looked to the past and, at the same time—by demanding a universal suffrage and annual Parliaments—to the future. Finally, it was conscious of the need to represent the interests of the new industrial towns and cities, (76).

During the revolutionary and Napoleonic wars (1793–1815), these various branches of the reform movement were stifled into only occasional activity by a widely held view that it was wrong to meddle with the constitution in the midst of a national emergency. It became easy to equate reform with treason, and societies like the London Corresponding Society were soon at pains to demonstrate their essentially moderate and patriotic purposes, (76). However, after the peace of 1815, the movement in all its parts—parliamentary and extra-parliamentary—burst into new life and was considerably assisted by the sharper analysis of society that became widespread as the full effects of the industrial revolution were felt. Furthermore, reform unions sprang up which relied upon a particularly sharp definition of class interests and to which reform meant the achievement of specific legislative ambitions rather than the restoration of any lost constitutional 'purity'. The Birmingham Political Union was one of the most important of these extra-parliamentary groups, and sought to unite the middle and working classes in order to achieve a parliamentary reform. Such a reform, it hoped, would enable parliament to deal more effectively with those economic factors upon which those classes depended for their future, (77). Other unions, such as the one in Huddersfield, merely expressed a kind of class solidarity, (78).

Needless to say, parliamentary reform was achieved in 1832 because of a complex combination of circumstances and not solely because of a demand from outside parliament. The state of party politics, whig ambitions and the economic crisis all played their part. However, it would be hard to deny the part played by the political unions in applying pressure; document (79) illustrates how this was done at a particularly crucial stage of the events of 1830–2.

76 The London Corresponding Society

This society was one of several devoted to parliamentary reform which sprang up in different parts of the country in the wake of the French Revolution and the publication of the first part of Thomas Paine's *The Rights of Man*. It was founded early in 1792 by Thomas Hardy, a Scottish shoemaker who worked in Piccadilly, and who wrote the memorandum, (a) below, outlining his ideas for a society and the rules (b) which should govern its activities. It should be noticed that the rules included the provision for a subscription of 1d per week—a sum designed to attract the artisans of the city.

(a) *The memorandum*

It has been a long and very just complaint that the people of this country are not equally represented in Parliament. The present Duke of Richmond boldly asserted that the majority of the Representatives of the whole nation are chosen by a number of voters not exceeding twelve thousand in his ... letter to Col. Sharman, Chairman of the Committee of Correspondence assembled at Lisburn in Ireland in August 1783. Many large and populous towns have not a single vote for a representative such as Birmingham containing above 31,000 of inhabitants, Manchester above 28,000, Leeds near 20,000 besides Sheffield, Bradford, Wolverhampton, Hallifax etc., according to Dr. Price. These facts are self evident (and) therefore need no comment. Let us look at this metropolis and see what a great majority of its inhabitants have not a vote. A parliamentary reform is that which of all other things in our opinion most deserves the attention of the public. We are more and more convinced from every days experience that the restoring the right of voting universally to every man not incapacitated by nature for want of reason, or by law for the commission of crimes, together with annual elections, is the only reform that can be effectual and permanent. As Providence has kindly furnished man in every station with faculties necessary for judging of what concerns them, it is somewhat strange that the multitude should suffer a few with no better natural intellects than their own to *usurp* the important power of governing them without control. The views and intentions of this society are to collect the opinions of all the unrepresented of the people as far as possible for they certainly are the persons agrieved. [They] therefore have the greatest right to stand forward like men for their privileges and if they are rejected [stand firm against those] who dare oppose them in their determination.

   (b) *Rules and Resolutions of this Society*

1. That a Society be instituted and called by the name of 'The Corresponding Society of the unrepresented part of the people of Great Britain'.

2. That this Society be unlimited in its numbers while there is one in Great Britain unrepresented and that no one shall be esteemed a member who has not paid at least one penny towards the expenses and continued weekly.

3. That as soon as twenty members are associated a general meeting shall be called when all the several laws or regulations already agreed to shall be read over and confirmed,

alter'd or annulled and at this meeting there shall be elected a President, Treasurer and Secretary.

4. That a committee be chosen to correspond with societies formed in different parts of Great Britian with the view of promoting the objects of this society.

5. That no person shall be proposed to be a member of this society unless he is recommended by one member and the proposal seconded by another.

6. That each member's name and place of abode be entered regularly in a book kept for that purpose.

7. That all proceedings of the society and its committee be fairly transcribed into proper books for that purpose by the secretary from the rough minutes against the next meeting of the society and the committee.

8. That no one be admitted a member under the age of twenty years nor any who has not resided in this country for one year.

BM Add. MSS 27811 ff 2–4.

————

The first meeting of the society was held on 25 January and by June the membership exceeded 1,000, the branches numbered at least a dozen and the central committee was in correspondence with many other societies around the country. However, the outbreak of war with France in February 1793 led Pitt's government to bring increasing pressure to bear on such societies. The LCS was fortunate to survive into 1795, but unfortunate to be charged by the government with the responsibility for the attack upon the King, on 29 October of that year, as he was making his way to open parliament. The declaration, (c) below, was a riposte to those charges, while the inquiry from Portsmouth (d) referred to the proclamation of the king, of 4 November, seeking to destroy societies like the LCS as well as the Treasonable Practices Bill introduced into the House of Lords on the 6th. The LCS replied that these measures were, in its view, a direct attack upon the liberties of the individual.

(c) *The declaration*

To the Parliament and People of Great Britain an explicit declaration of the principles and views of the London Corresponding Society, 23 November 1795. The London Corresponding Society feeling the awful importance of the situation in which their own efforts on behalf of liberty, and the arbitrary measures of an encroaching administration have conspired to place them—feeling also that the affairs of this long harassed and distracted nation have arrived at a most monumentous crisis—that the people and their oppressors are at issue, and that there is not but one alternative, Liberty and Reform, or Encroachment and absolute Despotism, conceive themselves called upon, once more, to appeal to that public so frequently warned by them and deluded by their calumniators and to state in the most clear and explicit terms the following Declaration of their principles.

1. This society is, and ever has been, most firmly attached to the principles of Equality, accurately defined and properly understood; but at the same time they regard with the utmost abhorrence, the base misrepresentations to which, for interested purposes these principles have been subjected. Social equality, according to its just definition, appears to them to consist in the following things:

i The acknowledgment of equal rights
ii The existence of equal laws for the security of those rights
iii Equal and actual representation, by which, and which alone, the invasion of those laws can be prevented; and such an administration of those laws insured, as will alike preserve the poor from the oppressions of the rich, and the rich from the insults and invasions of the poor.

In their ideas of equality, they have never included (nor, till the association of alarmists broached the frantic notion, could they ever have conceived that so wild and detestable a sentiment could have entered the brain of man) the equalization of property, or the invasion of personal rights and possessions.

This levelling system they know, and all rational men must immediately perceive to be equally unjust and impracticable; and they are ready to a man, not only to protest against, but to oppose, with their lives, every attempt of that description— attempts which they are well aware, instead of equalizing the condition of mankind, could only transfer property from its present possessors to plunderers and assassins of the most profligate description, and subject the nation to the brutal and ferocious tyranny of the most ignorant and most worthless of mankind.

2. With respect to particular forms and modifications of Government, this Society conceive, and ever have conceived, that the disputes and contentions about these which have so often distracted the universe (like bigotted attachments to particular forms of worship) are marks only of weak and inconsiderate minds, that in the pursuit of fleeting shadows forget the substance. Their attention has been uniformly addressed to more essential objects—to the peace—the social order—and the happiness of mankind; and these they have always been ready to acknowledge and believe might be sufficiently secured by the *genuine spirit* of the British Constitution. They have laboured therefore, with incessant application, not to *overthrow*, but to restore and *realize* that Constitution; to give practical effect to those excellencies which have been theoretically acknowledged; and to reform those corruptions and abuses which, though some have attempted to justify, no one has had the hardihood to deny.

Peaceful reform, and not tumultuary revolt, is their object; and they trust to the good sense and candour of the Nation that something more than *vague accusation* and *interested calumny* will be expected to discredit their protestation, that *They abhor alike* the FANATICAL ENTHUSIASM *that would plunge into a sea of anarchy in quest of speculative theories*; and the VILLANOUS HYPOCRISY *that would destroy the very essence of existing institutions, under pretence of preserving them from destruction*! ! !

3. This society has always cherished, and will ever be desirous to inculcate, the most decided abhorrence of all tumult and

violence, anxious to promote the *happiness* and therefore jealous of the *rights* of man they have never failed to propogate, nor to practice, the constitutional doctrine of opposing, by every peaceful and rational exertion, the encroachments of power and corruption. But they have never countenanced, nor ever will, any motion, measure or sentiment tending to excite commotion —to inflame the mind with sanguinary enthusiasm—or to extinguish the emotions of tenderness and humanity which ought particularly to characterise a free and enlightened nation.

At the same time, they do not wish to be understood as giving, by this declaration, any sort of countenance *to the detestable and delusive doctrines of Passive obedience and non resistance.* This is a system which none but *hypocrites* will *profess*, and none but *slaves* will *practice*. THE LONDON CORRESPONDING SOCIETY are neither the former, nor the latter; and on the alter of their own hearts they have *sworn—That no insolent encroachments of a corrupt and tyrannical administration—no dread of the last fatal arbitriment, shall ever compel them to be either.* They know that they have rights —they know that it is their duty to defend them—they know also, that to profess implicit submission is to invite oppression; and that to practice it is treason to posterity and sacrilege against nature . . .

Committee Room, Beaufort Buildings, 23 November 1795.

J. Ashley, Secretary.

(d) *A letter from Portsmouth to the Secretary of the LCS*

10 November 1795

Fellow Citizen,

We received yours and read it with great satisfaction. We are much obliged to you for your friendly communication and very excellent advice. We deferred returning an answer in order that we might inform you more particularly respecting our numbers —we now have about ninety and entertain no doubt of our further increase.

We wish citizens to have your opinion on the Proclamation and Bill now pending in the House of Lords; give us your advice. We are uneasy as we think it may greatly effect what liberty we now possess.

You may rest assured of our fidelity and firmness. We as a body are determined to abide by your decisions. Give us your advice freely and plainly—depend upon it we are True Friends.

We would wish to have an answer as soon as possible. We particularly request this as we conceive the Bill points directly at our meetings and under this persuasion have requested an attendance of all our members on Friday next. BM Add. MSS 27815 ff 14, 18.

77 Plans for a General Political Union

In the latter half of the 1820s, Britain was hit by a severe economic depression. This was one of the factors that encouraged the growth of political unions which sought parliamentary reform as a means of relieving distress and achieving social and economic reform. They varied considerably: both in composition—some being of an exclusively working-class character and others combining the middle and working classes—and in the remedies that they hoped would flow from a reform of the electoral system. The most important was the Birmingham Political Union, founded in December 1829, whose chairman and main inspiration was Thomas Attwood. Of this union, Professor Briggs has written, 'Class co-operation indeed was the basis of the Union, currency reform the economic philosophy and the ultimate object of action and parliamentary reform the means.' These attitudes were clearly stated in the plan of the BPU for a General Political Union read to a meeting of some 12,000 at 'Mr. Beardsworth's Horse and Carriage Repository' in Birmingham on 25 January 1830. The Bill of 1819 that is referred to enabled the Bank of England to resume cash payments and was designed to check the issue of paper currency.

The BPU Plan

The experience of the last 15 years, must certainly have convinced the most incredulous that the rights and interests of the middle and lower classes of the people are not efficiently represented in the Commons House of Parliament. A very few observations will be sufficient to place this important subject beyond the possibility of doubt.

In the year 1819, a bill was passed into law, under the assumption that it would add only *four per cent* to the national taxes and burthens. It is now very generally acknowledged that the bill thus passed into a law, has literally added *cent per cent*, to the national burthens; instead of *four per cent*, that has been literally *doubled*, or is in the undeniable process of *doubling*, the real weight, and the real value of every tax, rent, and monied obligation, in the kingdom . . . At three different periods, during the operation of this fatal measure, and now a fourth time, the industrious classes of the community generally, have been reduced to a state of distress which has heretofore been unexampled in its general extent and severity. At each of these periods, the profits of productive capital and industry have been destroyed, or so much reduced, as no longer to afford the just and necessary inducements to the employment of labour. The working classes of the country have thus been thrown generally out of employment, or they have been compelled to endure more labour than nature can support, or their fair and reasonable earnings have been sacrificed, in order to prevent the ruin of their employers.

Strange and unnatural as this state of things evidently is, it has, more than once, been attended with anomalies which have rendered it ten times more unnatural still. The markets have been glutted with food and clothing on the one hand, and with a hungry and naked population on the other. The most eminent parliamentary authorities have declared that the *loaves* have been too many for the *mouths*, and that the *mouths* have been too many for the *loaves*, *at the very same time*.

It is most certain, that if the rights and interests of the industrious classes of the community had been properly represented in Parliament, a general state of distress, attended with anomalies like these, would have commanded the instant attention of the House of Commons. *The cause* of the distress would have been ascertained, and the proper remedy would have been applied without delay. But what has been the conduct of the House of Commons? To this very day, the cause of these strange and unnatural, and distressful anomalies has never once been enquired into! . . .

Here then, we have *proof* that the rights and interests of the great mass of the community are not properly represented in Parliament. A triple proof has been added to every argument which has previously been drawn from reason and experience, that an effectual representation of the industrious classes in the Commons House of Parliament is alike necessary to the welfare of the people and the safety of the throne.

Nor is this state of things much to be wondered at, when the present state and composition of the Commons House of Parliament are considered. That honourable House, in its present state, is evidently too far removed in habits, wealth, and station, from the wants and interests of the lower and middle classes of the people, to have any just views respecting them, or any close identity of feeling with them . . .

But how is reform to be obtained? Is it reasonable to expect that the men whose ignorance and imbecility have caused the national injuries and distresses, should voluntarily reform themselves? The thing is not possible. What then must we do. Shall we have recourse to a vigour trenching upon the law? God forbid. Fortunately for us and for our country, the constitution has yet preserved to us some conservatory principles, to which we may have recourse, and by means of which we may hope that this great and vital object may be accomplished in a just, legal, and peaceful way . . .

Under these circumstances, therefore, it is necessary to form a general political union and organization of the industrious classes, and to appoint a political council, to inquire, consult, consider, and report from time to time, upon the legal rights which yet remain to us, and upon the political measures which it may be legal and advisable to have recourse to. It is necessary also, to provide permanent funds for the defrayment of the necessary legal expenses, which may be incurred, under the direction of the POLITICAL COUNCIL; for *money* is the *sinew of law*, and without great expense, no great objects can be secured ... A casual town's meeting now and then, without system, consistency, or permanency of object, or operation, and, perhaps, a county meeting at distant intervals, still more precarious and irregular, combined with dubious and generally delusive representations from the public press; these furnish, at present, almost the only means of bringing the constituent and legislative bodies into useful and efficient contact with each other. *Hence* the pernicious legislation under which the country now suffers. *Hence*, the innumerable acts of parliament, which are passed to day and repealed tomorrow, which are passed again on the third day, and again counteracted on the fourth, and which, whether passed or repealed, or counter-acted, or continued in force, have still a constant and encreasing tendancy to trench upon the rights of and interests of the industrious classes of the community. If those important classes of men had been properly protected by political union among themselves, if they had possessed political councils in all the great towns and districts, with ample funds at their commands, and with such intellect and integrity as their own ranks abundantly afford; under *these* circumstances, it would not have been possible for those innumerable acts to have been passed, which now *hem in* as it were, the rights and liberties of the subject on every side, and render it almost impossible for the *poor man* to *move* without *trenching upon a law*. Societies of this kind would have watched closely the proceedings of the legislature, they would have sounded the alarm on the approach of danger, they would have pointed out every rash, unjust, destructive or oppressive measure, the very moment it was first agitated; and there is no reason to believe that parliament would not have listened to remonstrances thus timely, constitutionally, and efficiently supplied.

The following then are the objects of the POLITICAL UNION.

1st.—To obtain by every just and legal means, such a REFORM in the COMMONS' HOUSE OF PARLIAMENT, as may ensure a REAL and EFFECTUAL REPRESENTATION OF THE LOWER AND MIDDLE CLASSES OF THE PEOPLE in that HOUSE.

2nd.—To enquire, consult, consider, and determine respecting the rights and liberties of the industrious classes, and respecting the legal means of securing those which remain and recovering those which are lost.

3rd.—To prepare Petitions, addresses, and Remonstrances to the Crown and Legislative Bodies, respecting the *preservation* and *restoration* of PUBLIC RIGHTS, and respecting the repeal of *bad laws*, and the enactment of *good laws*.

4th.—To prevent and redress as far as practicable, all LOCAL PUBLIC WRONGS AND OPPRESSIONS, and all LOCAL ENCROACHMENTS upon the rights, interests, and privileges of the community.

5th.—To obtain the repeal of the MALT and the BEER TAXES; and, in general, to obtain an alteration in the system of taxation, so as to cause it to press less severely upon the industrious classes of the community, and more equally upon the wealthy classes.

6th.—To obtain the *reduction of each separate tax and expense* of the Government in the same degree as the *legislative increase* in the *value of money*, has increased their *respective values*, and *has reduced* and *is reducing the general prices of labour* throughout the country.

7th.—To promote *peace*, union and concord, among all classes of His Majesty's subjects, and to guide and direct the public mind into uniform, peaceful, and legitimate operations: instead of leaving it to waste its strength in loose, desultory, and unconnected exertions, or to carve to its own objects, unguided, unassisted, and uncontrolled.

8th.—To collect and organize the peaceful express on of the

PUBLIC OPINION, so as to bring it to act upon the legislative functions in a just, legal and effectual way.

9th.—To influence by every legal means, the elections of
members of Parliament, so as to promote the return of
upright, and capable representatives of the people.

10th.—To adopt such measures as may be legal and necessary
for the purpose of obtaining an effectual Parliamentary
investigation into the situation of the country, and into
the cause of the embarrassments and difficulties; with
the view of relieving the NATIONAL DISTRESS, of rendering justice to the injured as far as practicable, and of
bringing to trial, any members of either House of
Parliament, who may be found to have acted from
criminal or corrupt motives. Birmingham Reference
Library, 313067; *Report* of the Birmingham Town's
Meeting, 25 January 1830.

78 The aims of the Huddersfield Political Union, 1831

Other unions did not possess such a specific set of objectives
as those expressed above. The Huddersfield Political Union,
for example, sent the following letter to Lord Wharncliffe, a
tory whose primary residence was situated just outside
Sheffield, on 1 November 1831.

My Lord,

With pleasure we inform you, that a committee has been
selected from the members of our Political Union, and that
arrangements are completed that they shall act in concert with
persons deputed from the surrounding hamlets, villages, and
factories for the express purpose of organising the whole
labouring population of this district.

We are proud to state, that the people have now sufficient
confidence in their own talents and energies, and are determined that no other class shall be entrusted (or ought to be
relied upon) to redress their wrongs or obtain their rights. The
age of the Demagogues is gone—Union, Caution, and deter-

mination of purpose is our Motto, while out most anxious wish
is that it may be yours! Too long have our faculties lain dor-
mant! Tyrants of every species have enslaved and insulted us!
A barrier against redress almost insurmountable has been
raised—a train of circumstances almost immoveable have been
formed. What remains then but for us to have recourse to our
only alternative, which is a general move in our whole strength
—to unite in one mighty phalanx! to request your co-operation
in the support of this Circular.

Our principal aim is to have delegates from such Societies
and places as may seem proper to send to such particular places
as shall be agreed upon, (we should say Manchester, as the
centre) to arrange a plan and frame general resolutions for a
grand meeting all over Britain and Ireland, on the same day
and hour, so that the people may come in all respects well
prepared to meet these tyrants on one great and general principle; display an irresistible front, steady in conduct and fixed
in purpose; demonstrating that one grand simultaneous movement is sufficient to renovate the most perverse state in which
society ever existed; and place it on an adamantine basis from
which no known power can remove it while the people are
awake to their rights. Wharncliffe MSS.

79 A pro-reform meeting organised by the Birming-
ham Political Union, 1832

The Reform Bill crisis of 1830–2 naturally excited the attention of all political unions. The defeat of the first and second
bills in 1831 led to widespread demonstrations, while the
rejection of the third in the House of Lords in May 1832 led
to the following protest meeting organised by the BPU on
7 May.

So early as Saturday the population of the town and its immediate districts began to evidence symptoms of great excitement,
and on Sunday the roads leading to Birmingham, but more
especially the northern roads, showed that the attendance from

distant parts of the country would be immense. Some thousands arrived in the course of that day; many of whom came from the extremities of the counties of Worcester, Stafford, and Glouces-ter. Before day-break, yesterday morning, all was bustle and preparation. The previous arrangements made by the Council were in themselves admirable, and executed with precision and punctuality by the various gentlemen to whom they were en-trusted. By eight, the persons appointed to conduct the Unions of the various towns of the neighbourhood that intended visiting the Meeting, repaired to their respective stations on the different roads, each mounted on horseback, and decorated, or distinguished, by a broad sash of office, embroidered with the Union Jack. As all the unions round the country had resolved either to attend in a body, or to send deputations, to the Meet-ing, a superintendent was appointed by the Council of the Birmingham Union to meet them on the different roads and to lead them, with other bodies, into the town. Between nine and twelve these various bodies began to enter Birmingham, all being preceded by bands of music, and exhibiting flags, upon which were inscribed various patriotic devices and mottos. At ten o'clock the Council, at which numerous gentlemen of consequence unconnected with the Association, assembled at the Unions' Rooms, in Great Charles-street, and all arrange-ments being completed, the procession, consisting of countless thousands, proceeded to Newhall-hill the place appointed for the Meeting. The spot fixed upon is a large waste piece of ground situated on the north side of the town, containing in size about six acres, and capable of accommodating, according to the most accurate calculation, the immense number of 150,000 persons. The ground rises on the front and on each side in the form of an amphitheatre, and taking into considera-tion the numbers who occupied the roofs of houses and various contiguous elevations, we should say, that not less than two hundred thousand persons were present. Shortly before 12 o'clock, the *programme* being all arranged, the immense multi-tude, headed by Thomas Attwood Esq., the Chairman of the

Birmingham Political Union, and the Founder of that and all other Unions, in company with the Council carrying white wands, and followed by an immense procession, proceeded by the Birmingham Union Band in their superb uniform, proceeded to the place of Meeting. We were favoured with a seat in the first carriage, but admirably situated as we were for viewing the whole of this most splendid cortege, we were unable to give anything like a description of the scene which it presented. Looking from the top of Mount-street in Newhall-street, to the end of the Great Charles-street, the spectacle, from the count-less myriads of which it was composed, and the splendid devices and colours which it exhibited, was truly magnificent. On the arrival of the members of the Union at Newhall-hill, the ground was found to be almost completely pre-occupied. With difficulty the cavalcade approached the waggons, allotted for the accommodation of the Speakers. The whole of the ground and the tops of the houses, as far as the eye could discover, appeared to be completely covered with human beings.

At appropriate distance, on the ridge of the hill, opposite the speakers, were various banners; amongst which in the centre, waved the Royal Standard, the same which was exhibited at Somerset House when the King went to open the New London Bridge. Among the almost innumerable flags, we noticed the banners of the Coventry, Warwick, Wolverhampton, Darlaston, Wednesbury, Walsall, Alcester, Bromsgrove, Studley, Stratford-upon-Avon, Redditch, and Shirley Unions. Our attention was, necessarily, in a great measure confined to one spot, but a gentleman who visited the several divisions, gives us the following particulars from personal observation. He estimates the Grand Northern Division, including Wolverhampton, Bilston, Sedgeley, Willenhall, Wednesbury, Walsall, Darlaston, and West-Bromwich, at 100,000 persons. The procession was four miles in length, the whole of the road, for that distance, being literally crowded. In this Division there were 150 banners, and 11 bands of music. The Grand Western Division, including Stourbridge, Dudley, Harborne, Craidley, Lye Waste, Oldbury, Rowley, Hales-Owen etc., was two miles in length, in numbers about 20,000, and exhibited 70 banners. The Eastern Division, including Coventry, Warwick, Bedworth, Kenilworth, Leamington and Stratford-upon-Avon, consisted of about 5,000, and exhibited 30 banners. The Southern Division, including Bromsgrove, Redditch, Studley, Worcester, Droitwich and Alcester, had 12 banners, 6 bands of music, and consisted of about 10,000 persons. The above estimates are exclusive of the immense numbers who attended the Meeting from Birmingham and its vicinity, which includes a population of about 150,000.

By twelve o'clock the vast cavalcade had reached the hustings. On Mr. Attwood's appearance he was greeted with loud and continued cheering. Birmingham Reference Library, 60732: *Report of the Proceedings of the Great Meeting* (7 May 1832).

Suggestions for Further Reading

ALTHOUGH the necessary research is in progress, there is no convenient work which provides the basic electoral statistics for this period. G. P. Judd's *Members of Parliament 1734–1832* contains notes upon all the Westminster MPs, but for election returns, constituency by constituency, one still has to consult the return to the House of Commons printed in 1878, *Members of Parliament 1213–1874*; this can be supplemented with H. Stooks Smith's *The Parliaments of England, Scotland and Ireland* (1844–50), which prints some of the polls. (Further research into polls is best pursued by referring to the handlist of surviving pollbooks prepared by the Institute of Historical Research, Senate House, London). This deficiency will, to a certain extent, be met with the publication of the volumes of the official History of Parliament, which cover the period 1790–1820. The three volumes already published, *The History of Parliament: The House of Commons, 1754–1790*, edited by Sir Lewis Namier and John Brooke, provide the statistics for that period; the substantial introduction (available as a separate publication), biographical entries and constituency histories give an authoritative interpretation of election politics in the later eighteenth century. It should be noted that a similar work for the Irish Parliament is being prepared by Dr A. P. W. Malcomson, of the Northern Ireland Public Record Office. There is still occasion, therefore, to consult T. H. B. Oldfield's *The Representative History of Great Britain and Ireland* (1816), which contains useful if often biased accounts of British and Irish constituencies; and J. Holladay Philbin's *Parliamentary Representation, 1832, England and Wales* (New Haven, Conn, 1965), which provides selected constituency information from 1826 to 1832.

The situation is rather similar with regard to works concerned more with interpretation than providing information. E. and A. G. Porritt's *The Unreformed House of Commons* (1903) is still the only work which attempts to deal with various aspects of electioneering in this as well as earlier periods. Although primarily concerned to discuss electoral politics in the context of notions about methods of representation, it throws a good deal of light upon social aspects. This work apart, the student has to choose from various books and articles. Sir Lewis Namier's *The Structure of Politics at the accession of George III*, although concerned with an earlier period is still an indispensable guide to both the parliamentary and social aspects of elections between 1784 and 1831. A similar but perhaps less defined approach is made in *The History of Parliament: The House of Commons, 1754–1790* to which he was a contributor. For detailed studies of particular constituencies and elections in Britain, the following articles can be consulted: N. Gash's 'Brougham and the Yorkshire Election of 1830', *Procs. Leeds Philosophical and Literary Soc.*, 8, 19–35; E. A. Smith's 'Lord Fitzwilliam and Malton', *English Hist. Rev.*, 80 (1965), 51–69, and 'The Yorkshire elections of 1806 and 1807', *Northern History*, 2, 62–90; D. Williams's 'The Pembrokeshire Elections of 1831', *The Welsh Hist. Rev.*, 1, 37–64; and R. Worthington Smith's 'Political organisation and canvassing in Yorkshire elections before the Reform Bill', *American Hist. Rev.*, 74, 1538–60. For a discussion of elections in a broader social and political context, M. I. Thomis's *Politics and Society in Nottingham, 1785–1835* is especially useful.

As far as Ireland before the Union is concerned, E. M. Johnston's *Great Britain and Ireland, 1760–1800* provides the most comprehensive treatment and, for a detailed study of one borough constituency, can be supplemented by A. P. W. Malcomson's 'The Struggle for control of Dundalk borough, 1782–1792', *Co. Louth Arch. Jnl.*, 17, no 1, 22–36. The post-Union period will be partially dealt with in the appropriate section of the *History of Parliament*, but students may like to consider Peter Jupp's 'Irish parliamentary representation and the Catholic vote, 1801–1820', *The Historical Jrnl.*, 10, 183–96, and 'Co. Down elections 1782–1831', *Irish Hist. Studies*, 18, no 69, the latter being specifically concerned to place elections in a sensible social setting. For the electoral activities of the Catholic Association, J. A. Reynolds's *The Catholic Emancipation Crisis in Ireland, 1823–29* is essential reading.

Not surprisingly, given the immediate attractions of the subject, a more comprehensive coverage has been given to the history of political groups operating outside the representative system. Still of considerable value are C. B. Roylance Kent's *English Radicals* (1899) and H. Jephson's *The Platform: its rise and progress* (1892); the latter is a very interesting work and deals with the relationship between politicians and popular opinion through the medium of the 'public platform'. G. S. Veitch's *The Genesis of Parliamentary Reform*, which charts the history of groups working for parliamentary reform, can now be read with a useful introduction by I. R. Christie, whose *Wilkes, Wyvil and Reform* supplements it, and provides a broader social and political setting for the reform movement from 1765 to 1785. For the climax of the parliamentary reform agitation, Asa Brigg's, 'The Background to the parliamentary reform movement in three English cities,' *Camb. Hist. Jrnl*, 10, 293–318, is essential. Finally, there is E. P. Thompson's, *The Making of the English working class*. As the title indicates, this book is mainly concerned to argue a thesis about the origins of class; it is therefore closely concerned with the need to relate political ideas and actions to social relations and circumstances.

Acknowledgements

THIS book has been assembled from a large variety of unpublished papers and with the generosity and guidance of a number of people and institutions. I would like to thank Mrs C. K. Adam, of Blair Adam, Fife; the Earl of Ancaster; the City Librarian of Sheffield City Library; Mr Paul Cassidi; the Marquis of Downshire; Earl Fitzwilliam and the Wentworth Estates Company; the Earl of Kimberley; the Earl of Lonsdale; the Viscount Melville; His Grace the Duke of Newcastle; His Grace the Duke of Norfolk; His Grace the Duke of Portland; Mr G. M. T. Pretyman; the Earl Spencer; the Trustees of the National Library of Scotland; the Trustees of the Chatsworth Settlement; the Earl of Wharncliffe, and His Grace the Duke of Wellington for allowing me to select for publication documents in their possession. I owe a special debt of gratitude to the libraries and record offices of Britain and Ireland for answering my impudent inquiries: in particular to the record offices of Bedford, Berkshire, Cornwall, Essex, Huntingdonshire, Hertfordshire, Northern Ireland and Wiltshire; and to the Birmingham Reference Library; the Grimsby Public Library; the Hereford City Library; the Leicester Museum and Reference Library; the Nottingham University Library; the National Library of Ireland; the State Paper Office, Dublin; and the National Library of Wales for allowing me to quote from manuscripts in their care. I would also like to thank my colleagues, M. J. Barnes and Dr J. Bossy; and Mr E. A. Smith, of the History Department, Reading University, for their advice and encouragement; and to record my gratitude to the late Professor Aspinall for entrusting me with transcripts of some of the documents in this collection and for his interest in my work.

PETER JUPP
Lecturer in Modern History,
The Queen's University, Belfast

Index